The authors

Damien Millet teaches mathematics to post-A-level classes preparing entrance exams to top Higher Education establishments. He lives in Orléans, and is the General Secretary of CADTM France (Committee for the Abolition of Third World Debt).

Eric Toussaint is a historian and political scientist, President of the CADTM, member of the International Council of the World Social Forum and of the Scientific Advisory Board of ATTAC France. He is the author of *Your Money or Your Life! The Tyranny of Global Finance* (1999), co-author of *Le bateau ivre de la mondialisation. Escales au sein du village planétaire* (2000), *Afrique: abolir la dette pour libérer le développement* (2001), *Cuba: le pas suspendu de la révolution* (2001) and *Sortir de l'impasse. Dette et ajustement* (2002).

Reading committee

Sylvie Bourinet is a former journalist and an active member of CADTM France.

Denise Comanne is an art historian and prime mover of the CADTM; co-author of *Femmes, enfants, face à la violence: résistance du Nord au Sud* (1999).

Stéphane Desgain works for the Centre National de Coopération au Développement (National Centre for Co-operation and Development), Belgium, and is a member of the organizing committee of ATTAC Belgium.

Damien Elisei is a physics student and a member of CADTM France.

Jean-Marie Harribey is Professor of Economics at the University of Bordeaux, author of *La démence sénile du capital* (2002) and a member of the Scientific Advisory Board of ATTAC France.

Alain Saumon is a geographer and President of CADTM France.

Patrick Silberstein is a publisher.

Arnaud Zacharie is a researcher for the CADTM, spokesman for and co-ordinator of the scientific network of ATTAC Belgium and the author of several books.

DAMIEN MILLET | ERIC TOUSSAINT

Who owes who?

50 questions about world debt

Translated by Vicki Briault Manus with
the collaboration of Gabrielle Roche

University Press Ltd
DHAKA

White Lotus Co. Ltd
BANGKOK

Fernwood Publishing Ltd
NOVA SCOTIA

Books for Change
BANGALORE

SIRD
KUALA LUMPUR

David Philip
CAPE TOWN

Zed Books
LONDON · NEW YORK

in association with

 CA**D**TM

**Comité pour l'Annulation de
la Dette du Tiers Monde**

Who owes who? 50 questions about world debt was first published in 2004 by

in Bangladesh: The University Press Ltd, Red Crescent Building, 114 Motijheel C/A, PO Box 2611, Dhaka 1000

in Burma, Cambodia, Laos, Thailand and Vietnam: White Lotus Co. Ltd, GPO Box 1141, Bangkok 10501, Thailand

in Canada: Fernwood Publishing Ltd, 8422 St Margaret's Bay Road (Hwy 3) Site 2A, Box 5, Black Point, Nova Scotia B0J 1B0

in India: Books for Change, 139 Richmond Road, Bangalore 560 025

in Malaysia: Strategic Information Research Development (SIRD), No. 11/4E, Petaling Jaya, 46200 Selangor

in Southern Africa: David Philip (an imprint of New Africa Books), 99 Garfield Road, Claremont 7700, South Africa

in the rest of the world: Zed Books Ltd, 7 Cynthia Street, London N1 9JF, UK and Room 400, 175 Fifth Avenue, New York, NY 10010, USA.

www.zedbooks.co.uk

in association with le Comité pour l'Annulation de la Dette du Tiers Monde (CADTM), 345 rue de l'Observatoire, 4000 Liège, Belgium

Copyright © CADTM, 2004
Translation copyright © Vicki Briault Manus, 2004

The rights of Damien Millet and Eric Toussaint to be identified as the authors of this work have been asserted by them in accordance with the Copyright, Designs and Patents Act, 1988.

Cover designed by Andrew Corbett
Set in FF Arnhem and Futura Bold by Ewan Smith, London
Printed and bound in the EU bu Cox and Wyman Ltd

Distributed in the USA exclusively by Palgrave Macmillan, a division of St Martin's Press, LLC, 175 Fifth Avenue, New York, NY 10010.

A catalogue record for this book is available from the British Library.
US CIP data are available from the Library of Congress.
Caladian CIP data are available from the National Library of Canada

ISBN 1 55266 151 2 pb (Canada)
ISBN 81 8291 001 3 pb (India)
ISBN 983 2535 42 5 pb (Malaysia)
ISBN 1 84277 426 3 hb (rest of the world)
ISBN 1 84277 427 1 pb (rest of the world)

Contents

5 Anatomy of the developing countries' debt 74

6 Ongoing moves to reduce the debt burden 88

7 Debt cancellation and suspensions of payment in the past 108

8 The case for cancelling the DCs' debts 117

Abbreviations

ATTAC	Association for the Taxation of financial Transactions for Aid to Citizens
DCs	Developing Countries
FAO	Food and Agriculture Organization (UN organization)
GATS	General Agreement on Trade in Services
GDP	Gross Domestic Product
GMOs	Genetically Modified Organisms
HIPCs	Heavily Indebted Poor Countries
IBRD	International Bank for Reconstruction and Development (World Bank group)
IDA	International Development Association (World Bank group)
IFIs	International Financial Institutions
IMF	International Monetary Fund
LDCs	Least Developed Countries
NEPAD	New Partnership for African Development
NGO	Non-Governmental Organization
OAU	Organization of African Unity (replaced by the African Union in 2002)
ODA	Official Development Assistance
OECD	Organization for Economic Co-operation and Development
OPEC	Organization of Petroleum-Exporting Countries
PRSP	Poverty Reduction Strategy Paper
SAP	Structural Adjustment Programme
SDR	Special Drawing Rights
TRIPs	Trade-Related Intellectual Property Rights agreement
UN	United Nations
UNCTAD	United Nations Conference on Trade and Development
UNDP	United Nations Development Programme
USSR	Union of Soviet Socialist Republics
WHO	World Health Organization
WTO	World Trade Organization

Introduction

For the last twenty years, despite their innumerable natural and human resources, the Third World countries have been milked dry. The repayment of a debt which has swollen to colossal proportions prevents the populations from satisfying their most basic needs. The debt has become a subtle mechanism of domination and a new method of colonization, hindering any sustainable human development in the South. The policies applied by the indebted governments are more often decided by the creditors than by the parliaments of the countries concerned. The limits of the so-called debt-reduction initiative, launched with great pomp by the G7, the IMF and the World Bank, were shown up by the largest petition ever known (24 million signatures collected between 1998 and 2000, co-ordinated by the Jubilee 2000 campaigns). A radically different approach needs to be adopted: purely and simply, cancelling the debt, which is immoral and often odious.

The authors provide answers to various objections. Once freed of their external debt, is there not a risk that the countries might fall back into the trap of unsustainable indebtedness? Would debt cancellation not give a second chance to corrupt and dictatorial regimes? Will it not be the tax-payers of the North who end up paying for the cancellation? The authors argue that debt cancellation is necessary but not sufficient, and must be accompanied by other measures such as the recovery of 'ill-gotten gains' and their restitution to the despoiled populations. They suggest alternative sources of finance, both local and international. They also ask: who owes what to whom? They support the demands for reparation put forward by social movements in the South.

In the answers to fifty pertinent questions, this book explains in clear, simple terms how and why the debt impasse has come about. Graphs, maps and charts are used to illustrate the responsibility of those who uphold neo-liberalism and its corporate-driven globalization – the international financial institutions, the industrialized countries and also the leaders of the South. The book gives details of the roles of the various actors, of how the debt-machine that the developing countries get enmeshed in functions, of possible solutions to the situation, of alternatives to indebtedness ... It exposes the different moral, political, economic, legal and ecological arguments underlying the demand for total and unconditional cancellation of the external public debt of the developing countries.

Please send us your comments at one of the following addresses:

Damien Millet, 17 rue de la Bate, 45150 Jargeau, France
dmillet@citoyen.net

or

Eric Toussaint, 1 rue des Jasmins, 4000 Liège, Belgium
international@cadtm.org

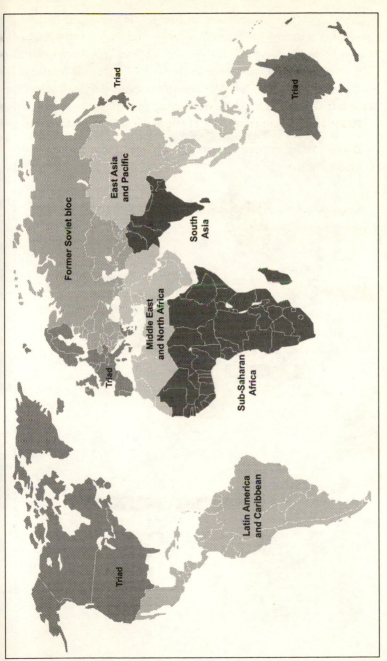

MAP 1 *The Triad and the six big regions of the developing world*

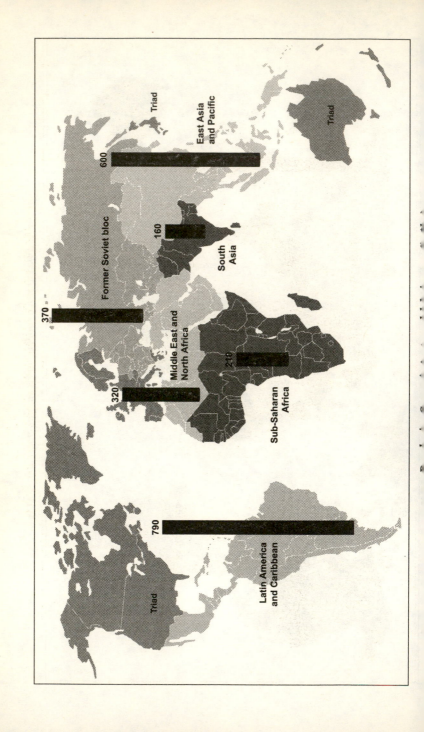

Triad

Former Soviet bloc

370

320

Middle East and
North Africa

600

East Asia
and Pacific

160

South
Asia

Sub-Saharan
Africa

210

Triad

790

Latin America
and Caribbean

Triad

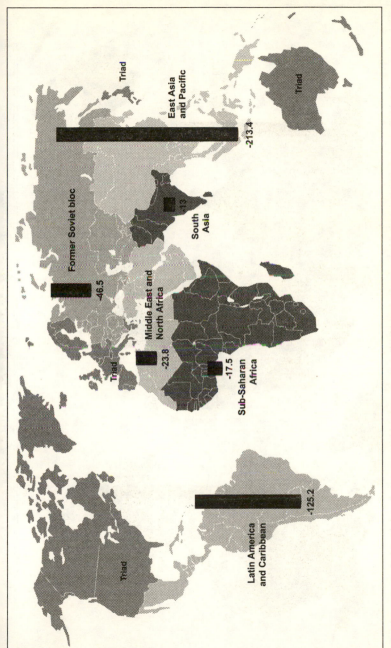

Triad

Former Soviet bloc

−46.5

Triad

Middle East and
North Africa

−23.8

Sub-Saharan
Africa

−17.5

South
Asia

−13

East Asia
and Pacific

−213.4

Triad

Latin America
and Caribbean

−125.2

MAP 3 *Net debt transfer, 1998–2001 (in $bn/cumulative total)*

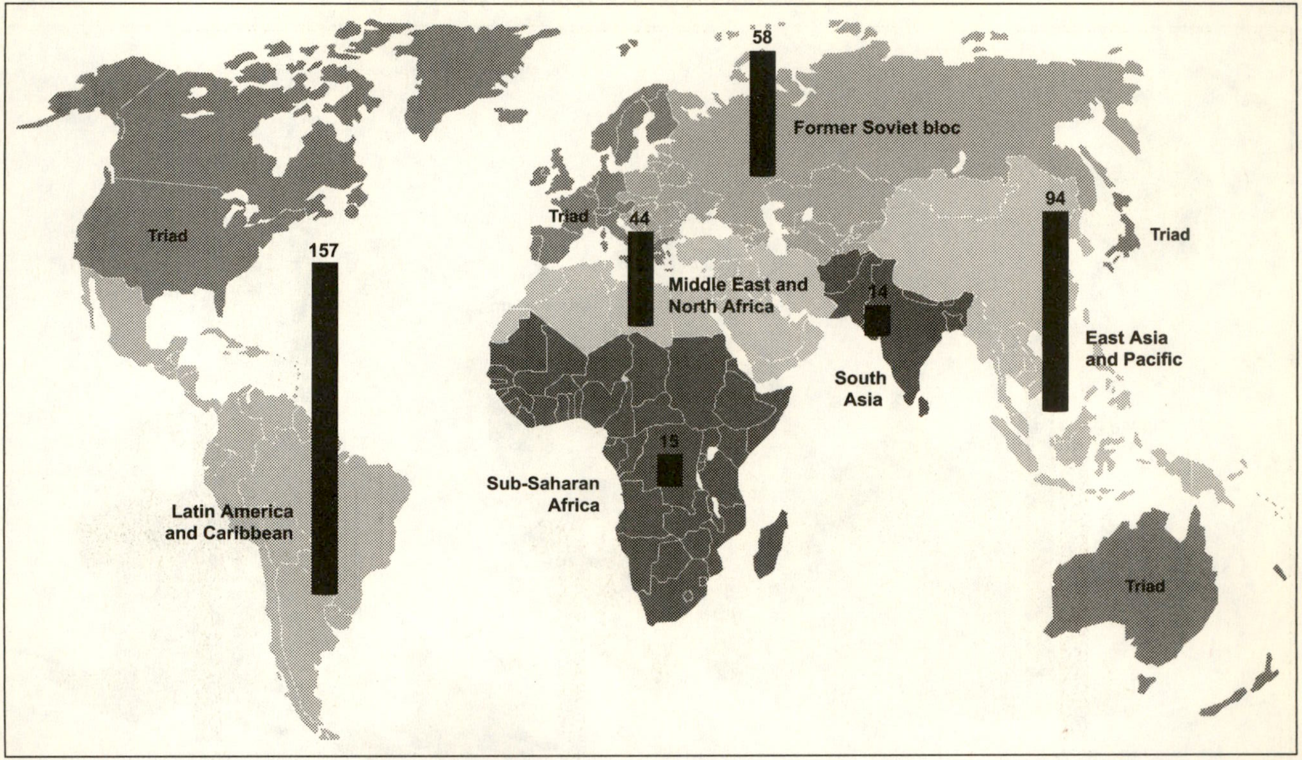

MAP 1 *Debt servicing by region, 2001 (total $382 billion)*

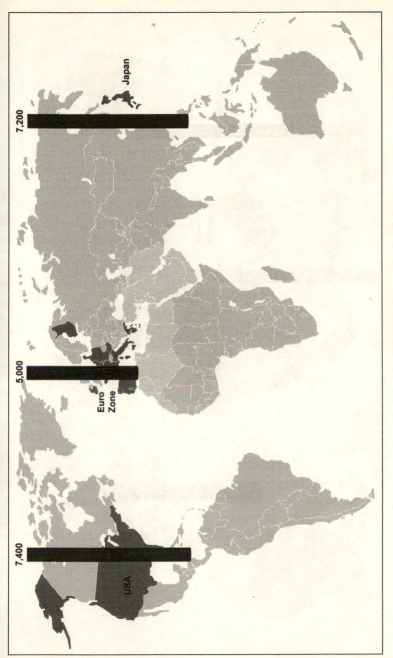

MAP 5 *Public debt of the Triad countries (in $bn)*

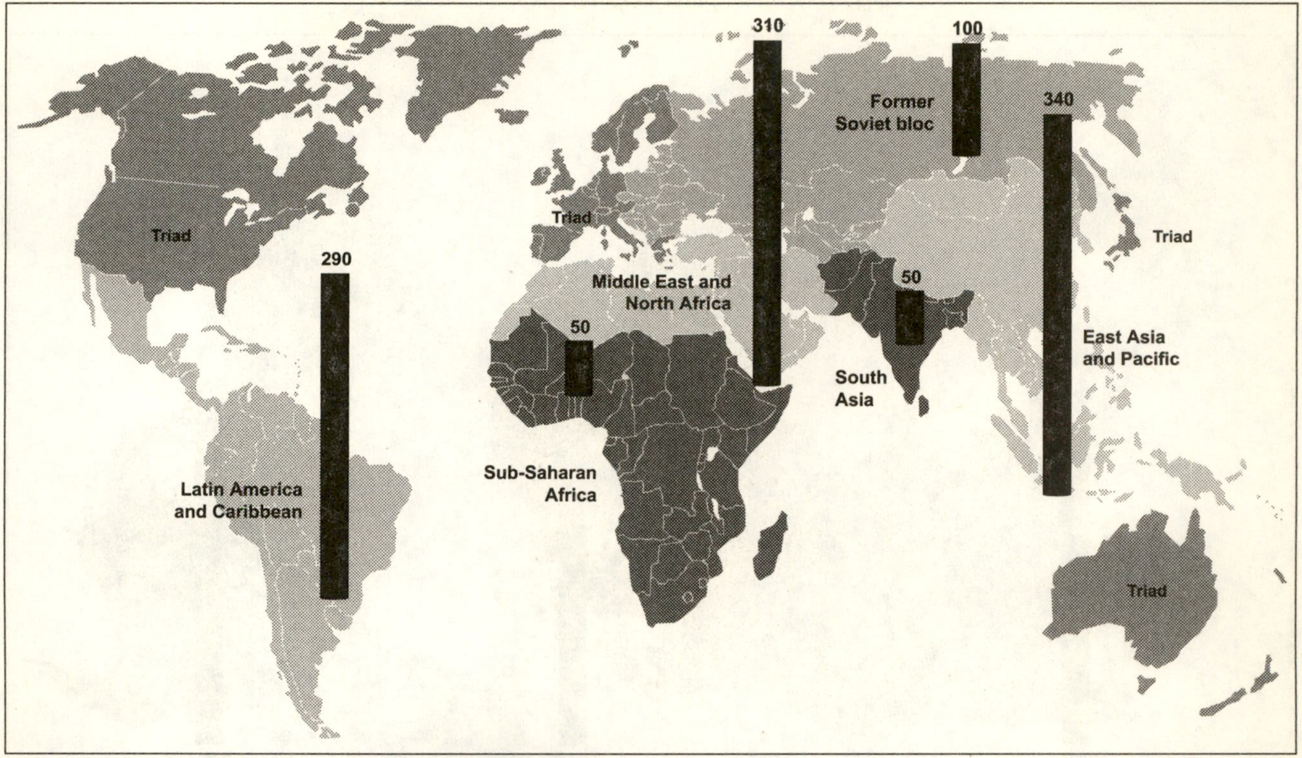

MAP 6 *Deposits made by the wealthy of each region in Northern banks (in $bn)*

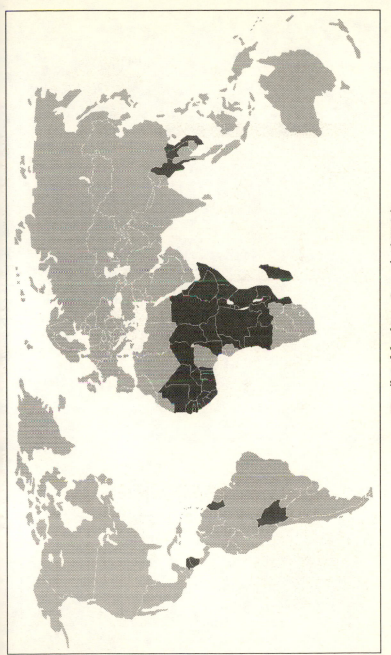

MAP 7 *Heavily Indebted Poor Countries (HIPCs)*

ONE

The Third World in the context of globalization

Q1 What is meant by the Third World?

First of all, the vocabulary used needs to be defined. The terms 'North', 'rich countries', 'industrialized countries' or 'Triad' all refer to the group formed by the countries of Western Europe, North America, Japan, Australia and New Zealand (*See* Appendix).

However debatable it may seem to group together such diverse countries as South Korea, Haiti, Brazil, Niger, Russia or Bangladesh in one category, we have adopted the terminology used in statistics provided by the international institutions. Thus we refer to all the countries outside the Triad as the Developing Countries (DCs). In 2001 there were 165 of these according to our figures. Within this category we distinguish, for historical reasons, between the countries of the former Soviet Bloc and the rest, classed as the Third World or the South.

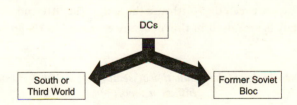

The Third World is divided into five regions: East Asia and the Pacific; South Asia; the Middle East and North Africa; Sub-Saharan Africa; Latin America and the Caribbean (*see* Appendix).

Out of a world population of approximately 6 billion people, the International Monetary Fund (IMF) (*see* Q12) estimates that about 86 per cent live in the Developing Countries.

The Gross Domestic Product (GDP; *see* Glossary) is the conventionally accepted indicator used to evaluate the production of wealth

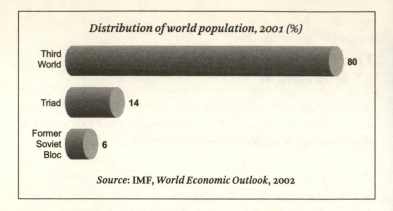

Distribution of world population, 2001 (%)

Third World 80

Triad 14

Former Soviet Bloc 6

Source: IMF, *World Economic Outlook*, 2002

in the world. However, the indication it provides is approximate and incomplete, with at least three major inadequacies:

• it does not take into account unpaid work, mainly provided by women
• the production of pollution is recorded as a positive and not a negative value
• the unit upon which the calculation is based is the price of a commodity or a service, and not the amount of work it requires

Despite these drawbacks, GDP is used as an indicator of economic imbalance between the North and the South. The GDP and all other monetary figures used in this book are expressed in US dollars, as

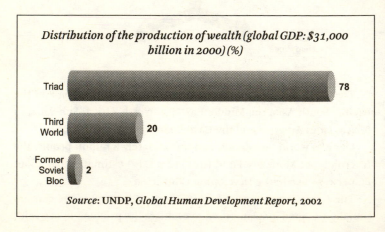

Distribution of the production of wealth (global GDP: $31,000 billion in 2000) (%)

Triad 78

Third World 20

Former Soviet Bloc 2

Source: UNDP, *Global Human Development Report*, 2002

more than 60 per cent of international loans and exchanges are transacted in this currency.

The production of wealth is largely concentrated in the North, and is in inverse proportion to the distribution of population. Present-day liberal globalization has been deliberately set up by the rich countries, which receive most of the profits, even though this can only be to the detriment of the 5 billion inhabitants of the DCs as well as large numbers of people in the industrialized countries.

> In 1951, I spoke in a Brazilian journal of three worlds, although I did not actually use the term 'Third World'. I invented and used that expression for the first time in writing in the French weekly *l'Observateur* on 14 August 1952. The article ended, 'for after all, the Third World, ignored, exploited and despised as was the Third Estate, also wants to be something'. I thus transposed Sieyes' famous words about the Third Estate during the French Revolution. *Alfred Sauvy, French economist and demographer* (trans. VB)

The GDP per inhabitant reveals the economic gulf that separates the North and the South. However, this provides only a very incomplete overview of the world economic situation, as it ignores the often flagrant income disparities within a given category of country. The

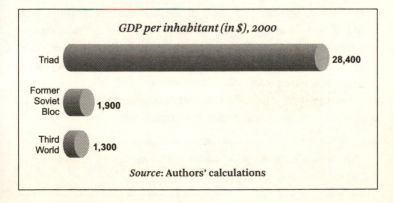

GDP per inhabitant (in $), 2000

Triad	28,400
Former Soviet Bloc	1,900
Third World	1,300

Source: Authors' calculations

3

One

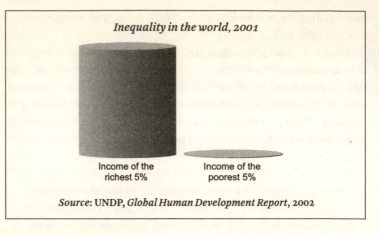

Inequality in the world, 2001

Income of the richest 5%   Income of the poorest 5%

Source: UNDP, *Global Human Development Report*, 2002

annual income of the richest 1 per cent of the world's population is equivalent to that of the poorest 57 per cent of the planet. Furthermore, the income of the richest 5 per cent of people in the world is 114 times higher than that of the poorest 5 per cent. Consequently, it is never useful to oppose North and South in overall terms.

The words are used only to express a geographical state of affairs; most of the decisions are made in the North and have heavy consequences for the DCs. However, within each region, the same mechanism of domination is reproduced. In the final analysis, and this is fundamental, the main problem is the oppression of one part of humankind (not exclusively located in the South) by another, much smaller in number but much more powerful. In other words, different interests (capital-holders) oppose the great majority of the population (wage-earners, small producers and their families) in both the North and the South – all those of us who are subjected to the present system. It is therefore crucial to make the correct analysis here in order to avoid misunderstanding some of the underlying issues and missing interesting alternatives.

Of course these extremely disparate economic situations tend to trigger off correspondingly dramatic human situations.

> You would help the poor, whereas I want poverty abolished.
> *Victor Hugo, Ninety-three* (trans. VB)

Q2 Are the living conditions of the poorest populations improving?

No, far from it. The living conditions of the most deprived have deteriorated almost everywhere over the last twenty years, though at different times, to different degrees and at different rates from one country to another. Some DCs were hit very early in the 1980s (Latin America, Africa, some countries of the former Soviet Union) while others were hit later, in the second half of the 1990s (East Asia). By the beginning of 2000, all the DCs were in a serious state of decline.

In 2000, at the United Nations' (UN) Millennium Summit, world leaders committed themselves to several calculated objectives – in reality far too modest – destined to reduce poverty by 2015. In its *Global Human Development Report*, 2002, the United Nations Development-ment Programme (UNDP) (*see* Glossary) shows how far there is still to go. It reckons that, 'For much of the world, the prospects are bleak', with at least a quarter of the world's population living in countries which will not manage to fulfil even half of the fixed objectives. Let us examine these in detail.

The millennium objectives

• *To reduce by half the proportion of the population living on less than a dollar a day* 2.8 billion people are estimated to be living on less than $2 a day; of these, 1.2 billion survive on less than $1 a day. Yet even these figures, given by the World Bank (*see* Q13) and the IMF (*see* Q12) are unreliable. A study by the United Nations Conference for Trade and Development (UNCTAD; *see* Glossary) of Sub-Saharan African countries showed that the figures provided by those two institutions considerably underestimated the true numbers of the poor. For example, whereas the World Bank estimated that the percentage of the population of Niger living on less than a dollar a day was 41.7 per cent, based on a survey of a sample of individuals, UNCTAD found more than 75 per cent, using the country's national accounts as their source.

Again according to UNCTAD, in the thirty-four Least Developed Countries (LDCs; *see* Glossary) in Africa, 65 per cent of the inhabitants live on less than $1 a day, and as many as 87 per cent on less than $2 a day. Often this amount of $1 is not nearly reached: many people in Niger, in the Democratic Republic of Congo, in Bangladesh, India or other DCs have to make do with less than $0.30 a day.

Furthermore, fixing the threshold of absolute poverty at $1 a day for Sub-Saharan Africa and $2 a day for Latin America is highly arguable. To give a more faithful picture of poverty, one would have to double, or even triple, current thresholds, which would give far higher results, more in keeping with the everyday reality of the great majority of the world's population. Finally, one would need to integrate non-monetary indicators such as the rates of access to education and healthcare, or life expectancy. This is what the UNDP is trying to do with the Human Development Rating (HDR; *see* Glossary) and the Human Poverty Index (HPI; *see* Glossary).

The fact remains that the World Bank estimates that a growth rate of 3.7 per cent per year per inhabitant is needed if the objective of reducing poverty by half by 2015 is to be reached. Yet more than 130 countries cannot possibly meet this. Indeed, fifty-two of them had negative growth rates during the 1990s, and poverty increased. In Sub-Saharan Africa, half of the inhabitants are poorer than in 1990 and the number of people living in extreme poverty has grown from 242 to 300 million over the past decade. It is expected to reach 345 million by 2015. It should here be emphasized that these figures are those provided by the World Bank which, as has been shown, underestimates the extent of poverty.

Even the growth rate of 3.7 per cent required to reduce poverty is valid only if the growth benefits everyone. Yet the inequalities in the world have reached a level described by the UNDP as 'grotesque'. According to statistics provided by seventy-three countries inhabited by 80 per cent of the world's population, forty-eight countries have seen the gap between rich and poor widen since the 1950s. Even in places where growth is considered satisfactory, it is the wealthy classes who get the most benefit, to the detriment of the poorest. The UNDP concludes: 'In view of current disparities, most countries are not recording a high enough growth rate to reach the objective fixed in terms of poverty.'

• *To reduce by half the proportion of the world's population suffering from hunger* In 2002, about 815 million people were suffering from hunger. Progress recorded in combating famine is far too slow. At this rate, it would take 130 years to eliminate hunger from the world, which is intolerable. The famines which appeared in the summer of 2002 in six Southern African countries were seized upon by the United States as a means of getting rid of 500,000 metric tonnes of genetically modified cereals. For the sake of the 13 million people threatened by starvation, the states of the region, especially Malawi, Lesotho, Swaziland, Mozambique and Zimbabwe, despite their early recalcitrance, decided to accept these genetically modified organisms (GMOs; *see* Glossary). Zambia alone refused. The occurrence of famine has thus become the opportunity for the United States and the agribusiness multinationals to impose their GMOs despite the risks to health and the environment, with no respect for the safety principle. In such a case, the South falls an easy prey to experimentation. The exports are in no way a structural solution to the famine problem since, at the same time, the DCs are reducing the production of staples (*see* Glossary) necessary for the survival of the local inhabitants in favour of cash crops for export to the North.

• *Provide all children with the means to have a complete primary education* Registration rates are slowly climbing but, in 2002, 133 million school-age children in the world did not go to primary school. As for reading and writing, the figures are very disappointing. Almost one adult in two in the LDCs is illiterate. Yet a good-quality educational system is essential if a country is to shed poverty in the long term.

• *To obtain educational equality between girls and boys and equality between the sexes, generally* Situations differ greatly, but out of the 854 million illiterate adults in the world in 2000, 544 million are women, and 60 per cent of children deprived of primary schooling are girls. Yet educating girls would have a positive impact on many aspects of daily life. Furthermore, flagrant inequalities exist between men and women at different levels of human development. The struggle for equality between the sexes must be a priority, first as a matter of principle and, even more so, because women play a dominant role in the improvement of family welfare.

• *To reduce child mortality by two-thirds* Each day, 30,000 children die of easily treatable diseases. For the UNDP, these children are 'the invisible victims of poverty'. Indeed, 'often, simple and easy-to-manage improvements in nutrition, health and hygiene infrastructures and education for mothers' would be enough to prevent these deaths.

In the Third World, an average of one child in four does not receive basic vaccines. In Sub-Saharan Africa, the rate rises to more than one child in two. This is why one child in six dies before the age of five. The UNDP reckons that eighty-one countries, inhabited by 60 per cent of the world's population, will not reach the objective fixed for 2015.

• *To reduce perinatal maternal mortality by three-quarter*s Each year, over 500,000 women die of complications related to pregnancy and childbirth

• *To eradicate the spread of AIDS* By the end of 2000, 22 million people had died of AIDS worldwide, and over 40 million individuals were infected by the virus, 75 per cent of whom were in Sub-Saharan Africa. In that part of the world, the epidemic causes 2.5 million deaths per year and infects one adult in twelve. In Botswana, one adult in three is infected, and the average life expectancy there will have dropped from sixty-five years in 2000 to thirty-one years in 2005. In Zimbabwe, it will have dropped from fifty-three in 2000 to twenty-seven in 2005. The other Southern African countries are similarly affected. In the case of seven of them, life expectancy has fallen below the forty-year mark. UNAIDS (the UN programme against AIDS) estimates that 10 billion dollars a year would be required to combat the disease efficiently, but in 2002 the DCs can only invest $2.8 billion. Meanwhile, the World Fund Against AIDS, Tuberculosis and Malaria, founded at the G8 (*see* Glossary) summit in Genoa in July 2001, is having trouble in raising funds. They received $750 million in 2002, and less than $500 million in 2003.

Although the human and social consequences are obviously a priority for us, the economic consequences are also disastrous. In Ivory Coast, AIDS medication for a sick person costs $300 a year, i.e.

somewhere between a quarter and a half of the annual revenue of an agricultural smallholding.

Pharmaceutical laboratories, backed by the states of the North, attempted to enforce patents, for their greater profit, by a scandalous law suit against South Africa in 2001. However, the Conference of Ministers of the World Trade Organization (WTO; *see* Glossary) in Qatar in November 2001, responded to public opinion by authorizing the production of more affordable treatments (generic drugs) using copies of original molecules. But as yet only a few countries (India, Brazil and Thailand) have a pharmaceutical industry capable of manufacturing them. What are the other countries to do if they cannot import anti-retroviral drugs?

• *Eradicate the spread of malaria and other widespread diseases* The ravages of malaria, especially in Africa, provide a significant example. The sums invested in research against malaria are feeble (less than $8 million a year) because the potential clients are often destitute and investors foresee only mediocre profits. Consequently, although promising solutions exist, malaria is again on the increase in Africa. In thirty years, the number of deaths has almost doubled. In 2000, malaria was the cause of a million deaths, 900,000 of which were in Africa; 700,000 of those were of children under five (one every forty-five seconds). The economic consequences are also extremely serious. According to the World Health Organization (WHO): 'Africa's GDP would be a 100 billion dollars more than it is today if malaria had been eradicated 35 years ago', and 'in Africa, malaria systematically hinders growth by more than 1% a year'. Furthermore, the report adds, a family with malaria 'spends on average more than a quarter of its income on anti-malarial treatments'.

Similarly, tuberculosis is the cause of 2 million deaths a year, mainly affecting the most poverty-stricken individuals, due to lack of access to treatment. By 2020, a billion people could be infected, meaning 35 million deaths.

In short, AIDS, malaria and tuberculosis are consuming the Third World, and most especially Sub-Saharan Africa.

• *To ensure the sustainability of environmental resources* Carbon

9

dioxide is the principal danger. Emissions have climbed from 5.3 billion tonnes in 1980 to 6.6 billion tonnes in 1998, mainly due to the rich countries. The Kyoto Agreement of 1997, aimed at reducing the emission of greenhouse gases, still has not been ratified by enough countries to become effective. The USA, which produces a quarter of the world's total emissions, even went so far as to withdraw its initial signature after the election of President George W. Bush. Indeed, his spokesman commented: 'A high consumption of energy is part of our way of life, and the American way of life is sacred.' The only signs of hope that this agreement, modest as it is, may one day become effective are the signatures of Russia, China and Canada, pledged at the Johannesburg World Summit on Sustainable Development in September 2002.

As far as deforestation is concerned, 250 million people living from agriculture are directly affected, and the survival of a billion human beings is at stake. Here again, it is the poorest who are the most at risk.

• *To reduce by half the percentage of people who do not have regular access to clean drinking water* In 2000, 1.1 billion individuals, i.e. nearly a fifth of the world's population, did not have access to a proper water supply.

• *To improve significantly the living conditions of at least 100 million slum-dwellers* In 2000, 2.4 billion people, i.e. two individuals out of five, had no proper sanitation. The consequences on health are serious. Every year, 4 billion people get diarrhoea and 2.2 million die from it.

• *To set up a global partnership for development* Official Development Assistance (ODA; *see* Glossary) provided by the North totalled about $51 billion in 2001, i.e. 0.22 per cent of the GDP of the rich countries (0.34 per cent for France; 0.37 per cent for Belgium; 0.34 per cent for Switzerland; and 0.11 per cent for the USA). In real terms, ODA decreased by more than 30 per cent between 1992 and 2002. Yet as long ago as 1970, the rich countries committed themselves to paying out 0.7 per cent of their GDP. Only five countries fulfil this objective today: Denmark, Luxembourg, the Netherlands, Norway and Sweden.

According to the UNDP, present ODA sums need to be doubled if the Millennium Objectives are to be met. This would still be less than what was promised in 1970. Despite all, the European Union does not plan to go beyond 0.39 per cent of its GDP by 2006. If this minimal commitment is all there is to be, there will be an inevitable lack of financial resources. Clearly, the fine speeches of the leaders of the North are failing to materialize into concrete acts.

After this worrying inventory of human development ...

According to figures published in the American *Forbes* magazine (February 2002), the accumulated fortunes of the 147 richest people in the world came to over $1,000 billion. In 1998 the fortunes of the 200 richest people had to be counted to reach this sum, and in 1995, those of the 358 richest people. Moreover, in 2002, the world's biggest seven fortunes together came to more than the GDP of the group of the forty-nine LDCs, with their 650 million inhabitants.

Still according to *Forbes*, the number of billionaires in the world is estimated at 497 (240 of whom inherited their fortune), and the cumulated wealth of these 497 billionaires comes to $1,544.2 billion.

Now in 2000, the UNDP and UNICEF calculated that $80 billion a

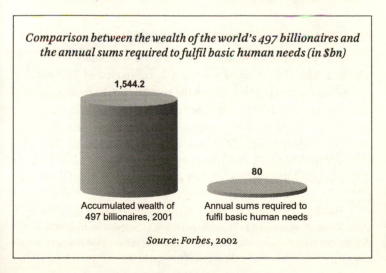

Comparison between the wealth of the world's 497 billionaires and the annual sums required to fulfil basic human needs (in $bn)

1,544.2

80

Accumulated wealth of 497 billionaires, 2001

Annual sums required to fulfil basic human needs

Source: *Forbes*, 2002

year for ten years would be enough to ensure that the entire population had basic services, such as decent food, access to drinking water, primary education and basic healthcare.

An annual contribution of 5.2 per cent levied on the fortunes of the 497 billionaires of this planet would suffice to guarantee all individuals the fulfilment of essential needs.

The UNDP's prognosis could not be clearer: 'In the absence of some spectacular change of tack, a generation from now, we truly run the risk of seeing the world's leaders fix the same objectives once again.'

How did things come to such a pass? Is it by pure chance, or the result of an iniquitous economic system? In the following pages, we will try to understand the mechanisms at work, so that we have a chance of bringing about the 'spectacular change of tack' that the UNDP has appealed for.

> When I give food to the poor, I am called a saint. But when I ask why the poor have nothing to eat, I am called a trouble-maker. *Dom Helder Camara, Brazilian Prelate, Archbishop of Recife 1964–85* (trans. VB)

Q3 What are the different kinds of debt?

Before examining the impact of debt, the vocabulary needs to be clarified. The total debt of a country is composed of *internal debt* (contracted with a creditor within the country, for example a national bank) and *external debt* (contracted with an outside creditor). A country's internal debt is often expressed in terms of the local currency.[1] To repay it, the state can, for example, print paper money, levy a tax or lower interest rates (*see* Glossary). It is an internal matter for the country concerned. This book will not deal with internal debt, even

---

1 Nevertheless, there are exceptions. In several countries, the internal debt, although expressed in national currency, is indexed on the dollar. Should the national currency be devalued, as was the case for Brazil in 2002, the internal debt automatically increases proportionately.

> I do not say that we should isolate ourselves as we have done in the past, but we are not trying to find out how to develop our country. We are trying to sell our country to foreigners for them to develop it in our stead. We are still in a colonial relationship whereby, in our own land, we Africans own nothing, control nothing, and manage nothing. Soon we will be foreigners in our own land. *Fred M'membe, Editor of The Post (Zambia) quoted in the Washington Post, 22 April 2002*

though it can weigh heavily on the debtors. As for external debt, it involves far more complex mechanisms, which can result in a real economic colonization. It is this that our attention will be focused on.

The external debt of the DCs can be broken down into *public* external debt and *private* external debt. The former is contracted by public bodies – the state, local authorities or public companies – or by private

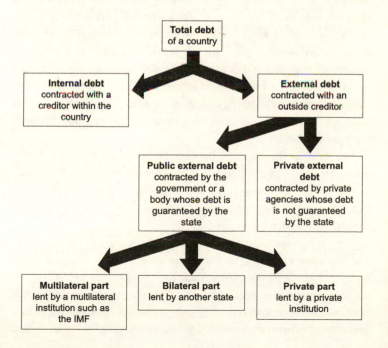

bodies whose debt is guaranteed by the state. The private external debt is contracted by private agencies, for example the subsidiary of a Northern multinational firm, and is not guaranteed by the state.

The external public debt can be broken down into three parts depending on the nature of the creditors. The multilateral part is that lent by a multilateral institution such as the World Bank or the IMF; the bilateral part is lent by another state; and the private part is lent by a private institution such as a bank or comes from the financial markets.

It is crucial to understand the vocabulary used. Total debt, external debt and public external debt must not be confused. The diagram on page 13 clarifies these terms.

Q4 What impact does the external debt have on human development?

The international financial institutions never cease to demand the repayment of the external debt. They place it as a priority in their pursuit of dialogue with the governments of indebted countries. We shall see that there are many reasons why the governments of the South could refuse what is often an immoral and illegitimate debt. Political, economic, social, moral, legal, ecological and religious arguments supporting this idea will be developed in this book. But the pressures exerted by the great money-lenders of the world and the collusion between the ruling classes of North and South are such that most leaders of DCs end up letting their populations bow beneath the burden of debt.

The debt in the DCs has become far too great for their fragile economies and has crushed all attempts at development. According to Kofi Annan, Secretary General of the UN, in 2000 debt-servicing (*see* Glossary) took up an average of 38 per cent of the budgets of Sub-Saharan African countries.

If governments follow the directives of the IMF, the World Bank and the other creditors, they have no choice but to instigate strict budgetary austerity measures. That means reducing public spending to a minimum in areas such as education, health, maintenance of infrastructures, and reducing public investment in projects that generate employment, in housing, not to mention in research and culture. The only areas where spending continues are the military, the police and the law.

Portion of budget allocated to basic social services and debt-servicing for the period 1992–97

Country	Social services (%)	Debt-servicing (%)
Cameroon	4.0	36.0
Ivory Coast	11.4	35.0
Kenya	12.6	40.0
Zambia	6.7	40.0
Niger	20.4	33.0
Tanzania	15.0	46.0
Nicaragua	9.2	14.1

Source: UNDP, *Global Poverty Report*, 2000

Governments have to procure US dollars (or other hard currency) in which the colossal debt repayments must be made. To do this, priority is given to export programmes: the accelerated exploitation of natural resources (minerals, oil, gas, etc.) and the frantic development of cash crops (coffee, cocoa, cotton, tea, groundnuts, sugar, etc.) Monocultures (*see* Glossary), particularly dangerous as they create a state of dependency in countries that are already severely deprived, are becoming the rule. Subsistence crops are abandoned, often with the result that countries that export agricultural produce have to import the foodstuffs they need.

In the battle for low production costs, no notice is taken of how the populations concerned manage to live or survive. Their social benefits are minimal and constantly under threat, and working conditions are deplorable.

Furthermore, the often abundant and varied natural resources of the DCs are overexploited, giving rise to grave environmental problems. According to some forecasts, the main natural resources of certain countries, for example oil in Gabon, will run out in a few decades. Many countries in the South are alarmed at the ravages of deforestation resulting from intensive logging of tropical hardwoods or the increase in size of the areas put to seed for crops. According to the UN's Food and Agriculture Organization (FAO), during the 1990s, these two factors caused the disappearance of over 94 million hectares of forest, almost exclusively in the DCs, in spite of the fact that in some regions the most vulnerable populations depend on the forest for their subsistence. Each year an area of forest the size of Hungary is destroyed. Worse still, at the UN, an International Peace Academy report claims that half the wood imported by the European Union was cut illegally in Africa by officially recognized companies. Lastly, the President of the World Bank reports that 12 per cent of bird species and 25 per cent of mammals will soon be extinct.

Fishing is another serious problem. A billion people in the world depend on fish as their primary source of protein, but total world catches have doubled in thirty years to reach 137 million tonnes in 2001. The FAO talks of 'sustained over-fishing' and estimates that catches need to be reduced by 30 per cent for fish stocks to be replenished. The situation is dramatic: the FAO reports that only half the world's fish stocks reach their biological age-limit and that 88 out of 126 species of marine mammals are threatened with extinction.

In an attempt to address these dire threats, 60,000 delegates from all over the world gathered in 2001 in Johannesburg (South Africa) at the World Summit for Sustainable Development organized by the UN. The cost of this disappointing High Mass was $80 million: $33 million was paid by private South African companies, and $45 million by the UN; $80 million represents 67 per cent of the annual health budget of Mali.

At this stage of the analysis, the relationship between debt and human development is clear. The debt mechanism enables the international financial institutions, the states of the North and the multinationals to take control of the economies of the DCs and to lay hands on their resources and wealth, to the detriment of the local populations. It is a new form of colonization regulated by the implementation of structural adjustment policies (*see* Q15 and Q16). Decisions concerning the South are not made by the South, but in Washington (in the US Treasury, or at the head offices of the World Bank or the IMF), in Paris (at the head office of the Paris Club [*see* Glossary], the group of the creditor states of the North [*see* Q17]), or

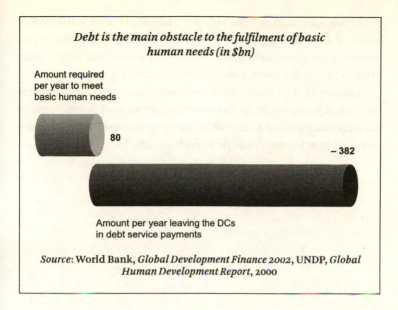

Debt is the main obstacle to the fulfilment of basic human needs (in $bn)

Amount required
per year to meet
basic human needs

80

– 382

Amount per year leaving the DCs
in debt service payments

Source: World Bank, *Global Development Finance 2002*, UNDP, *Global Human Development Report*, 2000

in the London Club (which represents the big banks of the North and does not always hold its meetings in London [*see* Glossary]). This is why the fulfilment of basic human rights is not given priority. The priority is to satisfy economic, financial and geopolitical criteria, such as debt repayment, opening up borders to capital and merchandise, privileged treatment for countries allied to the Great Powers or suffocation for 'enemy' countries (such as Cuba).

Just as cultivated and well-informed Frenchmen knew what their troops were doing in Vietnam and Algeria, cultivated and well-informed Russians knew what their troops were doing in Afghanistan and cultivated and well-informed South Africans and Americans knew what their 'auxiliaries' were doing in Mozambique and Central America, so today, cultivated and well-informed Europeans know how children die when the whip of the debt cracks over the poor countries. *Sven Lindqvist, Exterminez toutes ces brutes [Exterminate all those brutes]* (trans. VB)

In 2001 the total amount repaid by the DCs to service their debts came to $382 billion. These costly repayments deprive the DCs of precious resources to combat poverty efficiently, and at the same time aid from the North has constantly decreased.

Today it is clear that debt is the main obstacle to the fulfilment of basic human needs, at the heart of a system of domination by the rich countries of all the DCs. It is this mechanism, subtle and perverse as it is, that needs to be understood.

TWO

The origins of the developing countries' (DCs') debt

Q5 What were the main factors leading to the indebtedness of the DCs?

After the Second World War, the United States drew up the Marshall Plan (*see* Glossary) for the reconstruction of Europe. It massively invested in the European economy to help it get off the ground, and the European countries fast became privileged trading partners. More and more dollars were in circulation round the world. The US government tried to discourage the conversion of dollars to gold (which was possible until 1971), to prevent their stock of gold from drying up. They encouraged investment in American companies abroad, to avoid an excess of dollars returning and rocketing inflation (*see* Glossary). This is why European banks in the 1960s were flooded with dollars (known as 'Eurodollars'). They then began making loans on very favourable terms to the countries of the South which wanted to finance their development, especially the newly independent African states and the Latin American countries with their high growth rates. It will soon become apparent that the borrowers' motives were sometimes a long way from a desire to develop their countries.

From 1973, the increase in oil prices (known as the 'oil crisis') brought in comfortable revenues to the oil-producing countries which in turn placed them in Western banks. The banks offered to lend these 'petrodollars' to the countries of the South, with the incentive of low rates of interest. All these loans from private banks constitute the private part of the external public debt of the DCs.

To these were added the loans from the Northern states which, in 1973–75, following the oil crisis, underwent their first general recession since the Second World War. It was hard to find takers for goods manufactured in the North because of the slump and the beginning of mass unemployment. The rich countries then decided to endow the South with buying power so that they would buy goods from the North. This was the reason for the loans from state to state, often in the form of export credits or tied aid, as if to say, 'We will lend you $10 million at a low rate of interest, provided that you buy $10 million worth of goods from us.' This is how the bilateral part of the external public debt was constituted.

The third actor in the process of indebtedness is the World Bank. This institution, founded in 1944 at Bretton Woods (along with the IMF; *see* Q12 and Q13), considerably increased its loans to the Third World from 1968, under the presidency of Robert MacNamara, former US Defense Secretary during the Vietnam War. From 1968 to 1973, the World Bank granted more loans than during the entire period from 1945 to 1968. It incited the countries of the South to borrow massively to finance the modernization of their export apparatus and to draw them more tightly into the world market. These loans constituted the multilateral part of the external public debt.

Lastly, the governments and ruling classes of the South played an important role during this period. They listened to the song of the Western sirens and plunged into much deeper indebtedness for their countries. They often saw their way to skimming off for themselves money borrowed in the name of the state (or, How to Transform Part of the Debt into the Private Accumulation of Wealth).

Until the end of the 1970s, indebtedness remained sustainable for countries of the South because interest rates were low and the loans enabled them to produce more, to export more, and thus to earn hard currency to repay the debt and to invest.

Development as seen by the World Bank between 1968 and 1980

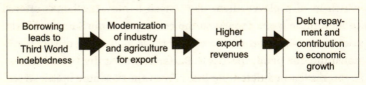

Borrowing leads to Third World indebtedness → Modernization of industry and agriculture for export → Higher export revenues → Debt repayment and contribution to economic growth

These four parties (private banks, states in the North, the World Bank, and governments in the South) are at the root of the exponential increase in the external debt of the DCs. Between 1968 and 1980, it was multiplied by twelve, going from $50 billion to $600 billion.

> In many countries debt strangles the public purse – and is often for money spent unproductively long ago, by authoritarian regimes. UNDP, *Global Human Development Report*, 2002

Q6 What is the geopolitical context of the over-indebtedness of the DCs?

After 1945 and the start of the Cold War, the two superpowers (the USA and the USSR) moved towards massive arms stocks and indirect confrontation, each with the intention of preserving and expanding its zone of influence. The initiative was taken by the USA when it created NATO in 1949. In the 1950s and 1960s, numerous countries were tempted by their own particular political experiments. After a relentless struggle, first Asian then African countries managed to bring about their decolonization. Some of those countries were determined to proceed along their own chosen paths to development, and to move away from the former colonial powers. They convened for the first time in 1955 in Bandung (Indonesia). The conference marked the emergence of the Third World on the international scene and was the prelude to non-alignment.

The World Bank took action to counter Soviet influence and various nationalist and anti-imperialist initiatives. This action was in the financial sphere. As the French Deputy Yves Tavernier put it in the 2000 Report of the French National Assembly's Finance Commission on the activities and surveillance of the IMF and the World Bank, the World Bank's role 'was to win over Third World custom, to the advantage of the Western world'. It was a two-edged strategy: the loans would be used both to support allies and to bring recalcitrant countries under control.

On the one hand, the World Bank supported the United States' strategic allies in different regions of the world (Mobutu in Zaire from 1965 to 1997; Suharto in Indonesia from 1965 to 1998; Ferdinand Marcos in the Philippines from 1965 to 1986; the Brazilian dictatorship from 1965 to 1980; Augusto Pinochet in Chile from 1973 to 1990; the generals Videla and Viola in Argentina from 1976 to 1983, and so on) to strengthen the zone of American influence.

On the other hand, the World Bank granted conditional loans to the countries that were trying to implement policies which did not comply with the dominant capitalist model. It would offer them the capital they needed, telling them that the export of the raw materials they produced would be enough to cover both repayments and the modernization of their industrial base. By this means the World Bank acquired the right of inspection over the economic policies practised in countries of the South, and strove to halt the development of independent policies and to bring a number of leaders who were moving away (Gamal Abdel Nasser in Egypt from 1954 to 1970; Kwame N'Krumah in Ghana from 1960 to 1966, for example) back under the aegis of the great industrial powers.

When any leaders of the South declined the offer, the Northern powers did not hesitate to overthrow them and to replace them with dictators (the assassinations of Patrice Lumumba in the former Belgian Congo in 1961; of Sylvanus Olympio in Togo in 1963; of Salvador Allende in Chile in 1973) or to organize military intervention (US interventions in Santo Domingo in 1965, in Vietnam, in Cuba through the intermediary of mercenaries in 1961; French interventions in Gabon in 1964 to restore Léon M'ba to power, in Cameroon several times during the 1960s in support of the government of Ahmadou Ahidjo, in Chad several times since 1960, in the Central African Republic in 1979 to instal David Dacko after a putsch; as well as many others). When such actions fall through, as was the case with Fidel Castro who has been in power in Cuba since 1959, the country is ostracized from the community of nations – once again a high price to pay.

In many cases, during the Cold War, loans were destined to corrupt governments. The issue was not whether the money was improving a country's welfare, but whether it was leading to a stable situation, given the geopolitical realities of the world. *Joseph E. Stiglitz (Chief Economist of the World Bank, 1997–99, Nobel Prize for Economics, 2001), on French televison in the programme L'Autre mondialisation [The Other Globalization] Arte, 7 March 2000* (trans. VB)

The geopolitical facts thus form the backdrop to the process of indebtedness of the countries of the South.

Q7 Who were the actors in the indebtedness of the countries of the South, and how have the loans been used?

The populations benefited hardly at all from the loans contracted by the leaders of the countries of the South. Most were contracted by dictatorships who were the strategic allies of the great powers of the North. One has only to study the list of the most heavily indebted countries in 1980 to find numerous, often authoritarian, regimes with close political ties to the Triad: Brazil, Mexico, South Korea, Argentina, Indonesia, Algeria, Turkey, Egypt, the Philippines, Chile, Pakistan, Peru, Nigeria, Thailand and so on.

A sizeable proportion of the sums borrowed was embezzled by corrupt regimes. They were all the readier to lead their countries into debt as they were able to skim off commissions for themselves with the complicity of the other instigators of indebtedness. How is it that, when he died, Mobutu, who had ruled Zaire for over thirty years, left a fortune estimated at $8 billion, equivalent to two-thirds of his country's debt? Not to mention the accumulated wealth of those close to him. And how is it that in Haiti, in 1986, the external debt came to $750 million when the Duvalier family, who had ruled for thirty years (first François – known as Papa Doc – then Jean-Claude, known as Baby Doc), fled to the French Riviera with a fortune estimated at more than $900 million? How else to explain the newly acquired wealth of the Suharto family in Indonesia, whose fortune, when they were routed in 1998 after reigning for thirty-two years, was estimated at $40 billion, at a time when the country was in a deep depression?

Sometimes, as in the case of the Argentine dictatorship (1976–83), the situation is ludicrous. During that period, the debt was multiplied by 5.5, reaching a total of $45 billion in 1983, mainly contracted with private banks, with the agreement of the American government. As of 1976, an IMF loan gave a clear signal to the banks of the North: the Argentine dictatorship was respectable. The junta in power undertook to force public companies into debt, such as the oil company YPF whose external debt rose from $372 million to $6 billion, i.e. a sixteen-fold increase in seven years. But hardly any of the hard currency borrowed at that time ever reached the coffers of the public companies. The sums borrowed from US banks were largely replaced in the same in the form of deposits, at a lower rate of interest than that of the loan. Large commissions then contributed to the personal enrichment of those close to the dictatorship. For example, between July and November 1976, the Chase Manhattan Bank received monthly deposits of $22 million on which it paid interest at 5.5 per cent. At the same time and at the same rhythm, Argentina's Central Bank (*see* Glossary) was borrowing $30 million from the same bank at a rate of 8.75 per cent. All this took place with the active support of the IMF and the United States, maintaining the regime of terror, while Argentina and the USA drew closer after the nationalist experiment of Peron and his successors.

> From 1976 to 1983, the policy of indebtedness and loans was totally arbitrary. This implicates the staff and executive boards of public and private institutions. The existence of an explicit link between the external debt, the flow of foreign capital in the short term, the high interest rates on the internal market and the corresponding sacrifice of the national budget after 1976 cannot have escaped the notice of the IMF authorities who were supervising economic negotiations at that time. *Sentence of the Federal Court of Argentina, 14 July 2000* (trans. VB)

This was how the debt increased very fast, as did the personal wealth of those close to the dictatorship. It was also profitable for the banks of the North. Part of the money came back into their coffers, and could be loaned again to others who also repaid with interest. Moreover, the wealth of the dictators was very useful to the banks as it served as a guarantee. If the government of an indebted country were to show any ill-will over repayment of debts contracted in the name of the state, the bank could quietly threaten to freeze the secret personal assets of its leaders, or even to confiscate them. Corruption and the ensuing embezzlement have thus played an important role.

Furthermore, the money which did reach the borrower country was put to a very specific use. Priority was given to financing huge energy or infrastructure projects (dams, power generators, roads, railways), very often inappropriate or megalomaniac, and nicknamed 'white elephants'. The aim was not to improve the daily life of the local populations, but rather to extract the natural resources of the South and transport them easily to the world markets. For example, the Inga Dam in Zaire made it possible, from 1972, to instal a high-voltage power line 1,900km long to the mineral-rich province of Katanga, with a view to its exploitation. Yet no transformers were installed along the way to provide the villages below it with electricity.

Other, often overweening, dam projects have been made possible by finance from the North: Kedung Ombo in Indonesia, Bhumibol and Pak Mun in Thailand, High-Krishna and Sardar Sardovar in India, Tarbeta in Pakistan, Ruzizi in Rwanda, Yaceryta on the river between Argentina and Paraguay, Blabuina, Tucurui and Itaparica in Brazil.

The same logic still prevails regularly, as is borne out by the construction of the Chad–Cameroon pipeline, begun in the 1990s, to bring oil from the Doba region, an enclave in Chad, to the maritime terminal of Kribi (Cameroon), 1,000 km away. It is being built with a complete disregard of the interests of the local populations. For example, to begin with, the authorities responsible for the project, co-financed by the World Bank in partnership with Shell, Exxon and Elf, proposed compensation of 25 CFA francs (about 3.7 US cents) per square metre of groundnuts destroyed, 5 CFA francs (0.7 US cents) per square metre of millet lost, or 3,000 CFA francs ($4.5) per mango sapling destroyed, whereas according to the Chad Deputy, Ngarléjy Yorongar, a mango tree's first fruition alone can produce 1,000 mangoes, each of which fetches about 10 CFA francs (0.15 US cents).

Another example is China, which in 1994 began the construction of a gigantic dam at Three-Gorges, which will hold back a 600 km-long lake. The dam means displacing 2 million people and will do irremediable damage to the local ecosystem. Northern multinationals present there, such as Alstom, are not in the least fazed by the human rights abuses or the threat to the environment.

Buying arms or military hardware to oppress the population also partly accounts for the increase in indebtedness. Many dictatorships have kept their hold on power by buying arms on credit, with the passive or active complicity of the creditors. Today there are therefore populations repaying debts that were incurred for the purchase of arms used to kill their own people. Only consider the 30,000 'disappeared' of Argentina under the dictatorship (1976–83), the victims of the Apartheid regime in South Africa (1948–94) or the genocide in Rwanda (1994). The borrowed money also served to finance the dirty dealings of such regimes, to compromise opposition parties and pay for costly election campaigns and policies based on patronage.

Tied aid is another favoured use for loans. Here, the money is used to buy products manufactured by firms in the creditor country, and helps to adjust its trade balance (*see* Glossary). The real needs of the population of the DC take second place.

Infrastructures imposed by the multinationals of the North, tied aid, arms purchases for massive repression, embezzlement and corruption – this is what the borrowed money has been used for, for decades. Today, populations are being milked dry to repay a debt which never even profited them.

> Which bankers batted an eyelid when they saw that a loan destined for a Mexican or Philippine state company was in fact paid straight into the account in Boston or Geneva of a high-ranking state official? *Philippe Norel and Eric Saint-Alary, L'endettement du Tiers-Monde [Third World Indebtedness] 1988* (trans. VB)

The debt crisis

Q8 How can the debt crisis be explained?

After the Second World War, the early stages of development in the Third World were not completely subordinated to funding procedures controlled by banks and international institutions. Most of the capital flow from North to South during the 1950s and 1960s was of public origin. At that time, Third World subordination was mainly due to standard colonial practices which had not yet been abolished, or to a lack of control over the exploitation and pricing of the raw materials and agricultural products whose production and export they specialized in. This subordination was made manifest in two main areas: unfair exchange and the downgrading of the terms of exchange. Both problems have subsisted until the present day, aggravated by the spiralling debt mechanism.

All this changed in the 1970s when three factors converged.

The first was the crisis of capitalism which erupted in the form of reduced profitability of capital, the collapse in 1971 of the international monetary system founded in 1944 and the fall in the value of the dollar already undermined by the accumulation of dollars in the world (*see* Q5), then a fourfold increase in the price of oil in 1973. The big Western banks gradually found themselves saddled with an accumulation of dollars built up over several years because of the US balance of payments deficit (*see* Glossary) and suddenly further increased after the first oil crisis. For this reason, and just when growth in the industrialized countries was beginning to slacken off, the banks began a frenzied campaign to incite Third World countries to take up offers of loans on easy terms. Real interest rates were very low because of high inflation

The second factor is to be found in a crisis specific to the USA. At the end of 1979, it needed to get out of its financial crisis, combat high inflation and reassert its world leadership after a string of humiliating failures in Vietnam in 1975, and in Iran and Nicaragua in 1979. So the United States began an ultra-liberal U-turn, which Ronald Reagan continued when he was elected to the presidency. For several months, the United Kingdom, ruled with a rod of iron by Margaret Thatcher's government, had already initiated a harshly neo-liberal change of direction. Paul Volcker, the Director of the US Federal Reserve, decided on a large rise in US interest rates. For someone holding capital, this meant that it suddenly became very worthwhile to invest in the United States as it would bring in higher profits. That was indeed Volcker's intention: to attract investment to reduce inflation and revive the US economy (in particular by launching a huge military and industrial programme). Investors rushed in from all over the world. All over the world, under the influence of the USA, interest rates followed the same upward curve, with terrible consequences.

The interest rates on bank loans granted to states in the South were low, it is true, but variable and linked to the North American and British rates (actually indexed on the Prime Rate and the Libor, two rates fixed in New York and London). From about 4–5 per cent in the 1970s they rose to 16–18 per cent, and even more at the height of the crisis, as the risk premium (*see* Glossary) became huge. Thus, from one day to the next the countries of the South found themselves

Prices of certain raw materials and agricultural products between 1980 and 2001

Product	Unit	1980	1990	2001
Coffee (robusta)	cents / kg	411.7	118.2	63.3
Cocoa	cents / kg	330.5	126.7	111.4
Groundnut oil	$ / tonne	1,090.1	963.7	709.2
Palm oil	$ / tonne	740.9	289.9	297.8
Soya	$ / tonne	376	246.8	204.2
Rice (Thai)	$ / tonne	521.4	270.9	180.2
Sugar	cents / kg	80.17	27.67	19.9
Cotton	cents / kg	261.7	181.9	110.3
Copper	$ / tonne	2,770	2,661	1,645
Lead	cents / kg	115	81.1	49.6

Note: Prices in constant $ in 1990

Source: World Bank, *Global Development Finance 2002*

having to repay three times more. The rules were modified unilaterally; the indebted countries are caught in a 'trap'.

Moreover, the countries of the South were confronted with a third sudden change. The prices for the raw materials and agricultural products they exported fell. The great majority of loans had been contracted in strong currencies like the dollar. So during the 1970s, debtor countries had to procure more and more currency to repay their creditors. Conditioned to repay what they owed at all costs, they could see only one solution: produce more to export. In so doing, they flooded the market with ever-increasing amounts of coffee, cotton, cocoa, sugar, groundnuts, minerals, oil and so on, while the demand did not increase in the North. This caused a severe fall in prices, as the table on page 28 illustrates.

Thus the South had to repay more with less income. In the vice-like grip of the debt, it was impossible to meet the payments as they fell due. Countries had to get even deeper into debt in order to pay, but this time at high rates. The situation rapidly deteriorated.

What really happened

In August 1982, Mexico was the first country to announce that it was no longer able to repay its debts. Other heavily indebted countries, such as Argentina and Brazil, followed. This was the debt crisis which was to rock all the countries of the South, one after the other. The countries of Eastern Europe were not spared either, especially Poland and, a little later, Yugoslavia and Romania.

The debt crisis resounded like a great clap of thunder throughout the economic and political world. Not even the international institutions, whose job it is to regulate the system and prevent crises, saw it coming. A few months earlier, the World Bank had had no idea of what lay ahead, reporting in its *Global Development Report* for 1981: 'It will be more difficult for developing countries to manage their debts, however [tendencies] do not indicate a general problem.'

In short, the debt crisis had been caused by two phenomena which occurred in quick succession:

- the enormous increase in the amounts to be repaid, due to the sudden rise in interest rates decided in Washington
- the enormous price-drop for products exported on the world market by the indebted countries, the proceeds of which were to repay their loans, and also a halt in bank loans

All the indebted countries in Africa and Latin America (and, a little later, Asia), regardless of the type of government, the degree of corruption or of democracy, were confronted with the debt crisis.

It is crucial to identify the basic responsibilities. They are on the side of the industrialized countries (especially the US government and the bankers of the North). Corruption, megalomania and the lack of democracy in the South certainly made matters *worse* but were not responsible for *triggering* the crisis.

> The Latin American debt crisis in the 1980s was brought about by a huge increase in interest rates, a result of the Federal Reserve Chairman Paul Volcker's tight money policy in the United States. *Joseph Stiglitz, Globalization and Its Discontents, 2002*

Q9 How has the external debt of the DCs evolved over the last thirty years?

First let us recall that the debt was multiplied by twelve between 1968 and 1980. During this period, the expense represented by debt repayment was sustainable as long as interest rates remained low and export revenues were high. The situation changed drastically in 1980–81 due to the very high rise in interest rates imposed on the world by the United States and British governments on the one hand, and the fall in the prices of raw materials on the other.

The figures say it all (see CEPAL table opposite).

The amounts to be repaid greatly increased (because of very high interest rates) while export revenues fell, due to the sudden drop in the price of raw materials and basic agricultural products.

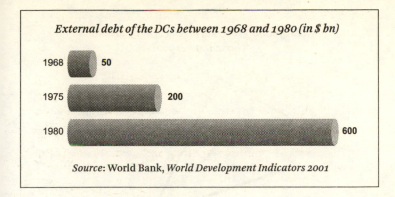

External debt of the DCs between 1968 and 1980 (in $ bn)

1968   50

1975   200

1980   600

Source: World Bank, *World Development Indicators 2001*

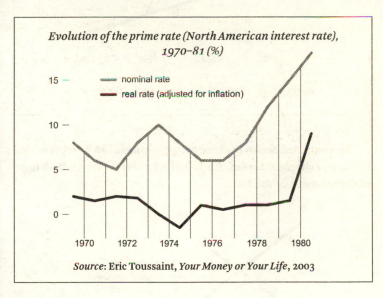

Evolution of the prime rate (North American interest rate), 1970–81 (%)

— nominal rate
— real rate (adjusted for inflation)

Source: Eric Toussaint, *Your Money or Your Life*, 2003

Year	Nominal rate (%)	Real rate (%) (minus inflation)
1970	7.9	2.0
1975	7.9	-1.3
1979	12.7	1.4
1980	15.3	1.8
1981	18.9	8.6

Source: CEPAL in Eric Toussaint, *Your Money or Your Life*, 2003

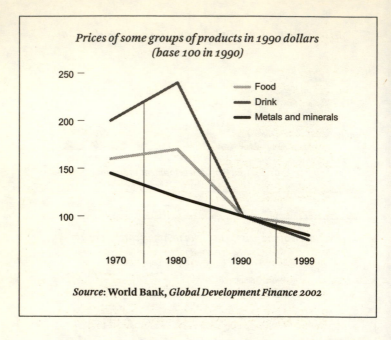

Prices of some groups of products in 1990 dollars
(base 100 in 1990)

Food
Drink
Metals and minerals

Source: World Bank, *Global Development Finance 2002*

The combined action of these two phenomena can be represented by the very simple diagram of a pair of scissors chopping off all hope of development at the base:

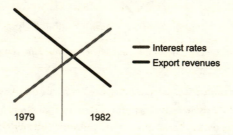

Interest rates
Export revenues

Since 1980, the external debt of the DCs has continued to rise: $600 billion in 1980, $1,450 billion in 1990, $2,150 billion in 1995, and about $2,450 billion in 2001. Its progress is charted below.

The slight fall between 1998 and 2001 can be explained in two ways: on the one hand, the variation in exchange rates between

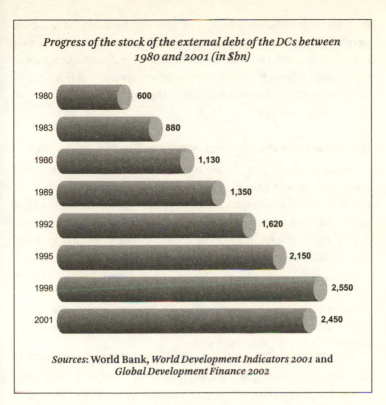

Progress of the stock of the external debt of the DCs between 1980 and 2001 (in $bn)

1980	600
1983	880
1986	1,130
1989	1,350
1992	1,620
1995	2,150
1998	2,550
2001	2,450

Sources: World Bank, *World Development Indicators 2001* and *Global Development Finance 2002*

currencies, in other words the variation in the dollar which is the counting unit used; and, on the other, the consequences of the Asian crisis in 1997, which spread to Russia and Brazil. Bank loans and

What development are we talking about? Are we talking about the corporate-driven model of development that leads to seventeen people dying of starvation every minute? Is it sustainable or unsustainable? Neo-liberalism is to blame for the disasters of our world. We do not put out the fire and we leave the pyromaniacs in peace. *Hugo Chavez, President of Venezuela, World Summit on Sustainable Development, quoted in Le Monde, 4 September 2002* (trans. VB)

The debt crisis

the issue of loan-bonds fell very low whereas the indebted countries were making enormous repayments, which led to a slight reduction in their debt stock (*see* Glossary). There is no indication that debt is falling off; far from it. It still remains at an unsustainable level. It is suffocating the DCs and condemning the majority of their inhabitants to abject poverty.

Q10 How have the creditors responded to the debt crisis?

When the debt crisis broke out in Mexico in 1982, then in the other Latin American countries, the creditors realized they were in an impasse and the world's financial system wobbled. The banks of the North were in danger because of the numerous loans they had made. For example, in 1982 the money owing from Brazil, Argentina, Venezuela and Chile represented 141 per cent of the Morgan Guaranty Bank's own capital assets, 154 per cent of that of the Chase Manhattan Bank, 158 per cent of that of the Bank of America, 170 per cent of that of the Chemical Bank, 175 per cent of that of the Citibank and 263 per cent of that of the Manufacturers Hanover. The bankers were in a critical situation.

Lenders were thin on the ground for a Mexico fallen on hard times and for the other states that followed suit. This is when the IMF intervened, on the decision of the governments of the rich countries. It made loans to enable the countries in crisis to manage to continue repaying their debts. To give them continued access to world capital, the IMF was in charge of setting up 'bail out' loans. The loan was made to a country with payment difficulties on condition the money borrowed be used to repay the banks and other private creditors. This is how the IMF saved the day for private lenders in the industrialized countries (*see* Q11). Next, it insisted on being repaid with interest. These policies were the result of blindly glorifying the market, that nothing must hinder, not even the cries of the hungry. The debt was ready to crush millions of individuals in its vice-like grip.

The rich countries, led by the United States, immediately took a series of initiatives to prevent the indebted countries from forming a united front, which was the last thing the rich countries wanted. Before any discussions could begin, they insisted that negotiations with indebted countries take place on a case-by-case basis, thus isolating each debtor country from the rest and keeping the upper hand.

As for the creditors, nothing could come between them.

- The World Bank and the IMF use a quota system whereby voting rights are proportionate to the financial contribution of each country (which means $1=1 vote). This gives the rich countries a comfortable majority with which to impose their views (*see* Q12 and Q13).
- Furthermore, the creditor states all belong to the Paris Club (*see* Glossary) through which they reschedule the bilateral part of the external debt of the states with repayment problems.
- The banks of the most industrialized countries belong to the London Club (*see* Glossary) which serves the same purpose regarding sovereign debt of the indebted states.

Thus a disproportionate power-balance was set up from the beginning of the debt crisis. For the last twenty years, the IMF, the World Bank, the Paris Club and the London Club have ensured its continuance in favour of the rich countries.

> Give me the control of a nation's currency, and I will not need to worry about those who make its laws. *Mayer Amschel Rothschild (1743–1812)*

FOUR

Management of the debt crisis

Q11 Who is the main actor in the management of the debt crisis?

Whenever one of its member-states is hit by a crisis, the IMF is always the first to intervene.

As soon as a country finds itself unable to continue its repayments, the IMF turns financial fire brigade; a strange sort of pyromaniac fire brigade, which fans the flames with its Structural Adjustment Programmes (SAPs).

Caught up in the debt-spiral, the DCs often have no other alternative than to take out new loans to repay the previous ones. The prospective lenders ask the IMF to intervene to guarantee the continuation of repayments. It accepts on condition that the country concerned agrees to follow the economic policy it dictates. These are the notorious IMF conditionalities, laid down in the SAPs (*see* Q15 and Q16). The borrower state's economic policies are now under the control of the IMF and its ultra-liberal experts. A new form of colonization comes into effect. There is no longer any need to maintain administrators and an army of occupation in the country in the old way, since the debt alone creates the conditions of a new dependency.

When an acute crisis arises (such as those of Mexico in 1982 and 1994, Southeast Asia in 1997, Russia and Brazil in 1998, Turkey in 2000, Argentina in 2001–02, Brazil in 2002 and so on), the IMF engages considerable amounts of money to keep the indebted country's creditors out of bankruptcy. For example, the IMF and the G7 loaned $105 billion to the Asian and Southeast Asian countries in 1997 (where the crisis, aggravated by the measures imposed by the IMF, led to 24 million people losing their jobs); the IMF loaned $31 billion to Turkey between the end of 1999 and 2002 (Turkey, a geo-strategic ally of the USA, near the oil and gas of Central Asia, and next to Iraq and Iran, thus became the IMF's biggest debtor in August 2002); over $21 billion to Argentina in 2001; $30 billion promised to Brazil for 2002–03 (to avoid contamination by the Argentine crisis and to tie down the new president elected in October 2002). However, these injected billions are never used to provide subsidies for basic necessities to help the poorest populations, nor to create jobs, nor to protect local producers. The IMF insists that creditors must be repaid as a matter of urgency. Moreover, these creditors are often the same private lenders who made speculative investments in the countries concerned then suddenly withdrew them, causing an aggravation of the crisis. Worse still, when private bodies suspend payments, the IMF and the World Bank often oblige the state to take on the debt, which amounts to getting the tax-payer to pay it off.

Thus, the amounts lent increase the debt of the borrower country, only to leave it immediately in the form of repayments to the creditors in the North. Since the IMF is in the habit of playing this role, creditors are prepared to take ever greater risks in their financial operations, knowing that in case of default by the borrower country, the IMF is there to bail them out, as a last-resort lender. This will be set off against a considerable increase in the external debt of the DCs concerned. The IMF works against the interests of numerous member countries it is supposed to help. This betrayal of its principles appears not to raise the slightest doubt: when the crisis comes, it never questions its prescriptions, never wonders whether its choices are perhaps misguided, but always accuses the indebted states of not having applied them rigorously enough. It is a crude procedure but it works.

Nearly 100 DCs have accepted or had to resign themselves to signing an SAP with the IMF. They then undertake to carry out ultra-liberal economic reforms which always follow the same plan: export more, privatize everything that can be privatized, remove all control

All obstacles to free trade will be removed, leaving companies free to produce and export their products as they wish and as the market decides. *Michel Camdessus, President of the IMF, 1987–2000, Indonesia, 1997, in L'Autre mondialisation, Arte TV, 7 March 2000* (trans. VB)

of capital movements, set high interest rates and spend less, often to the detriment of social budgets.

Q12 What does the IMF do?

The IMF was founded in 1944 in Bretton Woods (USA) on the initiative of forty-five countries, to stabilize the international finance system. In 2002, 184 countries belonged, East Timor being the newest member (joining in May 2002). Each country appoints a governor to represent it, usually the Minister of Finance or the governor of its Central Bank. The Board of Governors, the sovereign body of the IMF, meets every autumn. It deliberates over important decisions such as the admission of new countries or the preparation of the budget.

For the daily administration of IMF missions, the Board of Governors delegates its powers to the Executive Board, composed of twenty-four members. Each of the following eight countries enjoys the privilege of appointing a director: the United States, Japan, Germany, France, the United Kingdom, Saudi Arabia, China and Russia. The remaining sixteen are appointed by groups of countries. For example, the group formed by Austria, Byelorussia, Belgium, Hungary, Kazakhstan, Luxembourg, Slovakia, the Czech Republic, Slovenia and Turkey is represented by a Belgian director. This Executive Board, composed almost exclusively of men, generally meets at least three times a week.

The third governing body is the International Monetary and Financial Committee (IMFC) which is composed of the twenty-four governors of the countries on the Board of Governors. It meets twice a year (in the spring and the autumn) and has a consultative role in the IMF on the running of the International Monetary System.

The Board of Governors elects a managing director for five years. Contrary to democratic principles, a tacit rule reserves this post for a European. A Frenchman, Michel Camdessus, occupied the post from 1987 to 2000 and oversaw the enormous increase in the harmful effects of the IMF towards the most underprivileged countries. He was succeeded by the German Horst Köhler. The managing director manages a team of 2,650 higher officials from 140 countries, but is mainly based in Washington. The 'No. 2' at the IMF is always a representative of the United States, and in fact has considerable influence.

During the Asian crisis in 1997–98, Stanley Fischer, who had the post at the time, stood in for Michel Camdessus on several occasions. In the Argentine crisis of 2001–02, Anne Krueger, who was appointed to take over from Fischer by George W. Bush and his Secretary of State to the Treasury, Paul O'Neill, played a much more active role than Horst Köhler.

Since 1969, the IMF has had its own accounting unit which regulates its financial activities with its member-states, called Special Drawing Rights (SDR). Originally equal to $1, it is now re-evaluated on a daily basis from a selection of strong currencies (the dollar for 45 per cent, the yen for 15 per cent, the euro for 29 per cent and the pound sterling for 11 per cent). At the beginning of September 2002, 1 SDR was worth about $1.32. The total resources of the IMF came to 217.7 billion SDR (or $288 billion). If necessary, the IMF can borrow up to 34 billion SDR (or $45 billion) to complete its resources.

Unlike any democratic institution, the IMF has been endowed with a mode of operation similar to that of a corporation. Any country which joins the IMF has to pay an entry fee which is a *pro rata* share. Thus the country becomes a shareholder in the IMF since it contributes to its capital. This share is calculated according to the economic and geopolitical importance of the country concerned. Twenty-five per cent must be paid in SDR or one of the component strong currencies (or in gold, until 1978), and the remaining 75 per cent in the country's local currency. This has given the IMF a large stock of gold, as many countries paid their IMF subscription in the precious metal.

Furthermore, in 1970–71, South Africa, considered perfectly respectable by the IMF despite its continual violations of human rights under the Apartheid regime, sold it huge quantities of gold. In 2002 the IMF's gold reserves came to 103 million ounces (3,217 tonnes), valued at over $30 billion. These reserves do not enter into the IMF's loans; however, they confer upon the institution a stability and stature which are essential in the eyes of the players of international finance.

In 2002, the IMF's resources were divided between the equivalent of $157 billion which could not be used for loans (gold, weak currencies) and $131 billion usable (mainly currencies of the Triad countries), of which $43 billion were already committed and 88 billion still available.

These contributions from the member-states enable the IMF to lay down reserves which may be loaned to countries with a temporary deficit. Such loans are conditional upon the signing of an agreement stipulating the measures the country must take in order to get the money. These are the notorious Structural Adjustment Programmes. The money is made over by instalments, after verification that the stipulated measures have indeed been implemented.

As a general rule, a country in difficulty may borrow up to 100 per cent per annum of its share-value, up to a maximum of 300 per cent, except in the case of emergency procedures. These are short-term loans which the country is expected to repay as soon as its financial situation allows. The greater the share-value, the greater the amount which can be borrowed.

The interest rates on funding granted by the IMF to member countries can be calculated from the SDR's interest rate. In August 2002, the interest rate at which countries in difficulty could borrow from the IMF was 2.94 per cent. At the same time, the IMF was paying out interest on the sums loaned to it by the rich countries at a rate of 2.1 per cent. The difference enables the IMF to function on a daily basis.

Beyond this, the value of a country's share is the deciding factor on the influence it has (or does not have) within the IMF. The number of voting rights each country is entitled to results from a clever calculation based on its share-value. It corresponds to 250 votes plus one vote per 100,000 SDRs of the share. Unlike the United Nations where each country has one vote and only one (with the notable exception of the Security Council where five countries each have the right of veto), the system adopted by the IMF is $1=1 vote! Much closer to a corporation, there is nevertheless one significant difference: whereas a normal shareholder can decide to buy more shares on the stock exchange to increase his or her influence, a country may not decide to increase its share in the IMF to gain more influence within the institution. The only way of changing the distribution of the shares is the revision carried out every five years by the IMF itself, in which, as we shall see, the USA has a blocking minority. Thus the system is completely controlled by the biggest shareholders who guard their interests jealously.

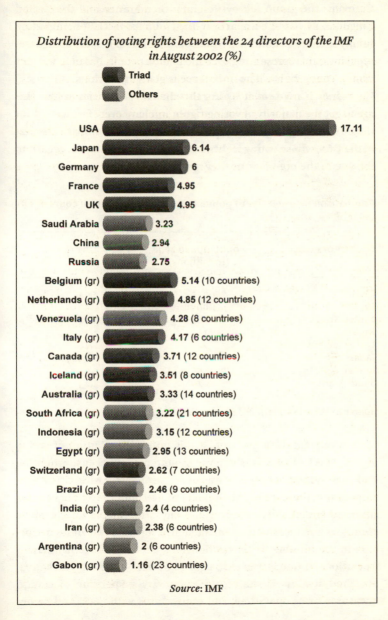

Distribution of voting rights between the 24 directors of the IMF in August 2002 (%)

Triad	
Others	

USA	17.11
Japan	6.14
Germany	6
France	4.95
UK	4.95
Saudi Arabia	3.23
China	2.94
Russia	2.75
Belgium (gr)	5.14 (10 countries)
Netherlands (gr)	4.85 (12 countries)
Venezuela (gr)	4.28 (8 countries)
Italy (gr)	4.17 (6 countries)
Canada (gr)	3.71 (12 countries)
Iceland (gr)	3.51 (8 countries)
Australia (gr)	3.33 (14 countries)
South Africa (gr)	3.22 (21 countries)
Indonesia (gr)	3.15 (12 countries)
Egypt (gr)	2.95 (13 countries)
Switzerland (gr)	2.62 (7 countries)
Brazil (gr)	2.46 (9 countries)
India (gr)	2.4 (4 countries)
Iran (gr)	2.38 (6 countries)
Argentina (gr)	2 (6 countries)
Gabon (gr)	1.16 (23 countries)

Source: IMF

Management of the debt crisis

The IMF's Executive Board accords the United States a place of honour (more than 17 per cent of voting rights), followed by Japan, Germany, the group led by Belgium, then France and the United Kingdom. By way of comparison, the group led by Gabon, including twenty-three Sub-Saharan African countries (French- and Portuguese-speaking) and representing over 140 million people, has only 1.16 per cent of voting rights. The imbalance is glaringly obvious.

With such a system, it is clear that the Triad countries easily manage to get the majority of voting rights and have every facility to pilot the IMF. Their power is utterly disproportionate if compared to that of the DCs, whose voting rights are ridiculously small with regard to the size of the populations they represent.

Comparison between size of population and voting rights of countries in the IMF

Country or group	Population in 2000 (in millions)	IMF voting rights (%)
China	1,275	2.94
India	1,009	1.93
United States	283	17.11
Russia	145	2.75
Group led by Gabon	140	1.16
Japan	127	6.14
France	59	4.95
Saudi Arabia	20	3.23

Sources: IMF; UNDP, *Global Human Development Report*, 2002

The scandal does not stop at this unfair distribution of voting rights. The United States enjoys absolute power because when the IMF was founded in 1944, it was in the strongest position. The USA managed to impose the requirement of a majority of 85 per cent for all important decisions concerning the future of the IMF, such as the allocation and the annulment of SDR, the increase or the reduction in the number of elected directors, decisions affecting certain operations or transactions with gold, how SDR should be evaluated, the modification of shares, the temporary suspension of certain measures or of operations and transactions with SDR, and so on.

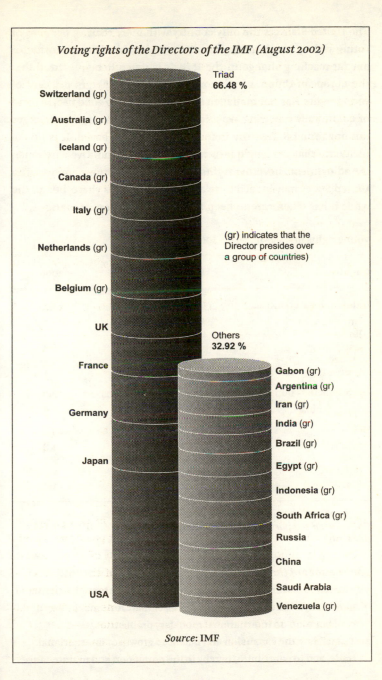

Voting rights of the Directors of the IMF (August 2002)

Switzerland (gr)

Australia (gr)

Iceland (gr)

Canada (gr)

Italy (gr)

Netherlands (gr)

Belgium (gr)

UK

France

Germany

Japan

USA

Triad
66.48 %

(gr) indicates that the
Director presides over
a group of countries)

Others
32.92 %

Gabon (gr)

Argentina (gr)

Iran (gr)

India (gr)

Brazil (gr)

Egypt (gr)

Indonesia (gr)

South Africa (gr)

Russia

China

Saudi Arabia

Venezuela (gr)

Source: IMF

Management of the debt crisis

The United States is the only country with more than 15 per cent of voting rights, which automatically gives it a blocking minority for any far-reaching change in the IMF. It is much to be regretted that the European Union, which could also put together 15 per cent of voting rights, has not managed to agree to put it to good use, instead of continually following Washington's lead. However, that changes nothing. The US Treasury is the only skipper on board. It is no co-incidence that the headquarters are in Washington. Over the years, the adjustments in voting rights have seen new nations emerge. The United States may indeed have agreed to reduce its share, but all the while it has taken care to keep it above the 15 per cent mark.

Voting rights in the IMF, 1945–2000 (%)

Country	1945	1981	2000
Industrialized countries	67.5	60.0	63.7
United States	32.0	20.0	17.7
Japan	–	4.0	6.3
Germany	–	5.1	6.2
France	5.9	4.6	5.1
United Kingdom	15.3	7.0	5.1
Oil-producing countries	1.4	9.3	7.0
Saudi Arabia	–	3.5	3.3
DCs	31.1	30.7	29.3
Russia	–	–	2.8
China	7.2	3.0	2.2
India	5.0	2.8	2.0
Brazil	2.0	1.6	1.4

Source: Yves Tavernier, *The French National Assembly's Finance Commission's Report on the Activities and Control of the IMF and the World Bank*, 2000

The missions of the IMF are carefully defined in its statutes

1   To promote international monetary co-operation through a permanent institution which provides the machinery for consultation and collaboration on international monetary problems.

2   To facilitate the expansion and balanced growth of international trade, and to contribute thereby to the promotion and maintenance

of high levels of employment and real income and to the development of the productive resources of all members as primary objectives of economic policy.

3 To promote exchange stability, to maintain orderly exchange arrangements among members, and to avoid competitive exchange depreciation.

4 To assist in the establishment of a multilateral system of payments in respect of current transactions between members and in the elimination of foreign exchange restrictions which hamper the growth of world trade.

5 To give confidence to members by making the general resources of the Fund temporarily available to them under adequate safeguards, thus providing them with opportunity to correct maladjustments in their balance of payments without resorting to measures destructive of national or international prosperity.

6 In accordance with the above, to shorten the duration and lessen the degree of disequilibrium in the international balances of payments of members.

In reality, the IMF's policies contradict its statutes. Contrary to point (2), the IMF does not give priority to full employment, whether in the highly industrialized countries or in the DCS. The IMF, under the influence of the United States' Treasury and with the support of the other highly industrialized countries, took the initiative of becoming a major actor, both politically and economically, in determining the policies of indebted countries. In this it has not hesitated to act in excess of its rights.

Surveillance, financial aid and technical assistance are the IMF's three areas of intervention. Yet, clearly, when one takes stock of the situation, it verges on total failure. Annual consultations with mem-

The IMF sees the end of the Asian recession as proof that its policies are right. That is stupid. All recessions come to an end. All the IMF managed to do was to make the Asian recession deeper, longer and more painful. *Joseph Stiglitz, in New Republic, April 2000*

ber countries and the recommendations of its experts did not enable the IMF to foresee and avoid any of the major crises of recent years. Some detractors hold that its policies even made them worse.

In February 2002, eighty-eight countries benefited from IMF loans in the name of financial aid, to the tune of $61.7 billion of SDR, or about $77 billion. The conditions that systematically accompany these loans reflect the extent of IMF control over the governments of the DCs.

As for technical assistance, it is brought to bear on public finances, monetary policy and statistics. In this area, the IMF is none too particular. It has given advice to the worst dictatorships.

> Somewhere between 'giving fish to the hungry', the prerogative of charity, and 'teaching them to fish', the cornerstone of development, the practice of 'leasing them costly and fragile fishing-rods 'seems to have slipped in, translating the new creed of the World Bank and the Monetary Fund. *Yves Tavernier, French MP, French National Assembly Finance Commission's Report on the Activities and Control of the IMF and the World Bank*, 2000 (trans. VB)

Q13 How does the World Bank operate?

The World Bank is the IMF's sister institution. Also founded in Bretton Woods in 1944, still boasting the same 184 members in 2002, its structure resembles that of the IMF in many points, but its mode of funding is different. Let us look at it in detail.

To aid Europe after the Second World War, the International Bank for Reconstruction and Development (IBRD) was founded. Its role evolved over time and it has become the official financier of the development of the DCs. This form of financing is based on highly dubious choices.

Four other bodies have since been formed, making up what is known as the World Bank Group. They are: the International Finance Corporation, set up in 1956 to finance the private sector of the DCs; the International Development Association, in 1960, for loans to the poorest countries; the International Centre for Settlement of Investment Disputes in 1966; the Multilateral Agency for the Guarantee of Investments in 1988 to encourage investment in the DCs.

The expression 'World Bank' includes the IBRD and the IDA. In 2002, it employed about 8,500 people in Washington and 2,500 more in its 100 offices throughout the world. Between 1945 and 2001, the World Bank lent about $360 billion to its different client countries.

As with the IMF, each member country of the IBRD appoints a governor to represent it. The Board of Governors meets once a year (in the autumn) and establishes its broad orientations.

The daily running of the Bank is assured by the Board of Directors, composed of twenty-four members and constituted on the same rules as the IMF. The sixteen groups of countries may, however, choose a representative of a different nationality from that of their IMF director. Note that France and the United Kingdom accomplished the great feat of appointing the same representative to the IMF's Executive Board as to the World Bank's, which is an indication of just how close and complementary these two institutions are.

The Executive Board elects a president for five years. The rule, as tacit as it is anti-democratic, reserves this post for a North American, chosen by the United States. The Executive Board simply ratifies this choice. Since 1995, the President of the World Bank has been James D. Wolfensohn. Formerly the Director of the Business Bank sector of Salomon Brothers in New York, he was born in Australia and had to become a United States citizen before being appointed to this strategic post.

> The potential for democratization of the global institutions remains considerable. Numerous proposals have been put forward to eradicate manifestly antidemocratic practices such as the right to veto in the United Nations Security Council and the selection procedure for IMF and World Bank leaders. *UNDP, Global Human Development Report, 2002*

The distribution of voting rights is also based on the $1=1 vote principle. Each of these rights corresponds to 250 votes plus one vote per portion of capital held, which gives a distribution similar to that effective in the IMF.

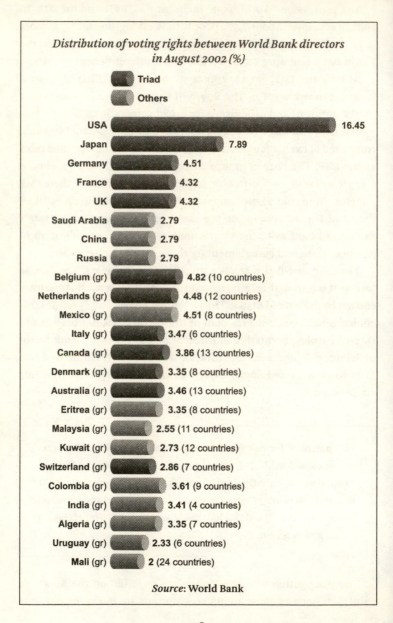

Distribution of voting rights between World Bank directors in August 2002 (%)

Triad
Others

USA	16.45
Japan	7.89
Germany	4.51
France	4.32
UK	4.32
Saudi Arabia	2.79
China	2.79
Russia	2.79
Belgium (gr)	4.82 (10 countries)
Netherlands (gr)	4.48 (12 countries)
Mexico (gr)	4.51 (8 countries)
Italy (gr)	3.47 (6 countries)
Canada (gr)	3.86 (13 countries)
Denmark (gr)	3.35 (8 countries)
Australia (gr)	3.46 (13 countries)
Eritrea (gr)	3.35 (8 countries)
Malaysia (gr)	2.55 (11 countries)
Kuwait (gr)	2.73 (12 countries)
Switzerland (gr)	2.86 (7 countries)
Colombia (gr)	3.61 (9 countries)
India (gr)	3.41 (4 countries)
Algeria (gr)	3.35 (7 countries)
Uruguay (gr)	2.33 (6 countries)
Mali (gr)	2 (24 countries)

Source: World Bank

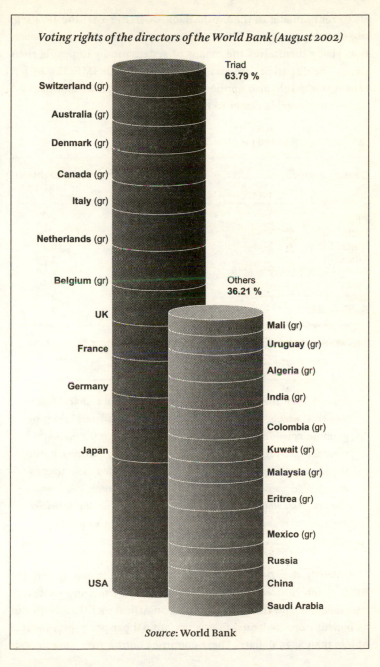

Voting rights of the directors of the World Bank (August 2002)

Triad
63.79 %

Switzerland (gr)

Australia (gr)

Denmark (gr)

Canada (gr)

Italy (gr)

Netherlands (gr)

Belgium (gr)

Others
36.21 %

UK

France

Mali (gr)

Uruguay (gr)

Germany

Algeria (gr)

India (gr)

Colombia (gr)

Kuwait (gr)

Japan

Malaysia (gr)

Eritrea (gr)

Mexico (gr)

Russia

China

USA

Saudi Arabia

Source: World Bank

Management of the debt crisis

To recapitulate: in the World Bank, as in the IMF, the DCs represent a tiny portion and the Triad countries have the lion's share, thus giving themselves the means of systematically imposing their views. The disparities are just as obvious as in the IMF. The 85 per cent majority rule also applies in the IBRD. So there, too, the USA wields considerable power to block decisions.

IBRD voting rights and number of inhabitants

Country or group	Population (in millions)	Voting rights in the IBRD (%)
China	1,275	2.79
India	1,009	2.79
United States	283	16.45
Russia	145	2.79
Group presided over by Mali	140	2.00
Japan	127	7.89
France	59	4.32
Saudi Arabia	20	2.79

Sources: World Bank; UNDP, *Global Human Development Report*, 2002

Some blame the Bank's dispersion on its main shareholder (the USA) which, in view of the reduction of its bilateral aid programme, considers the institution as a particularly useful instrument for exerting its influence in the developing countries. It can then be used as a source of funding to be accorded to its friends and denied to its enemies. *Yves Tavernier, French MP, French National Assembly Finance Commission's Report on the Activities and Control of the IMF and the World Bank, 2001* (trans. VB)

Officially, the IDA is just an association, but it is tied up with the IBRD which runs it. In 2002, it numbered 163 member-states, of which eighty (and thirty-nine of those in Africa) met the conditions to benefit from its loans, that is, an annual per per capita income of less than $875 dollars. These countries borrow over long periods (usually between thirty-five and forty years, with an initial deferral of ten years) and at very low interest rates (of around 0.75 per cent). The money comes from the richest countries, which reconstitute the IDA fund every three years.

The other DCs borrow from the IBRD at rates close to current market rates. The IBRD is careful to select profitable projects, just like a 'normal' bank. Whereas the IMF lends out money from shareholder countries, the World Bank gets the money it needs for these loans on the money markets. Indeed, the World Bank, guaranteed by the rich countries that are its biggest shareholders, is solid enough to get money at very good rates. Then the IBRD lends it out to the member countries, which repay the loans over a period of between fifteen and twenty years.

Being in a privileged position for borrowing from the markets enables the World Bank to set money aside for running costs and even to make a profit of about $1.5 billion a year.

Of the $17 billion of World Bank loans in 2001, more than half were made through the IBRD, i.e. $10.5 billion for ninety-one operations in thirty-six countries.

As indebtedness has grown, the World Bank, in conjunction with the IMF, has increasingly turned to actions aimed at producing macro-economic effects. Thus, the Bank is imposing more and more adjustment policies with a view to regulating the balance of payments of heavily indebted countries. The Bank does not hesitate to 'advise' the countries subjected to IMF therapy on the best ways to reduce budget deficits, to mobilize domestic savings, to encourage foreign investors to move in, or to liberalize exchange rates and prices.

Is it reasonable that the World Bank should be giving its support to private small-scale business projects for access to water and electricity, instead of contributing to the construction of public systems? Should the World Bank be financing private systems of health and education? *Yves Tavernier, French MP, French National Assembly Finance Commission's Report on the Activities and Control of the IMF and the World Bank, 2001* (trans. VB)

Lastly, and especially since 1998, the World Bank participates in financing the SAPs, by according ever larger structural adjustment loans to the countries that adopt its policies.

Q14 What is the logic behind the IMF's and the World Bank's economic policy?

The rich countries' reaction to the debt crisis in 1980–82 was to entrust the IMF and the World Bank with the job of imposing strict financial discipline on the indebted countries. This was based on two important tools: projects and Structural Adjustment Programmes (SAPs).

The projects, set up by the World Bank, consisted of making loans for precise objectives, such as building up the infrastructure (*see* Q7). Theoretically, this was to reduce the gap between the DCs and the highly industrialized countries. However, in practice, far from enhancing development of industries in the DCs, the projects chosen were those which integrated them in the global market to serve the interests of the multinationals of the North.

As for the SAPs, their first aim, according to the official doctrine, was to help states in difficulty to get back on their feet financially. For the international financial institutions, this was an absolute priority. To do it, the IMF and the World Bank insisted on opening up the country's economy to attract capital investment. The objective for states of the South which apply the SAPs is to export more and spend less.

These Structural Adjustment Programmes imposed on many indebted countries by the IMF and the World Bank are also known as the 'Washington Consensus'. Placing the emphasis on statistics instead of the human aspect, they have had and are still having terrible consequences for the populations and the economies of the South, as we shall see. Populations have been suffering ever greater privations over the last twenty years, poverty has increased with alarming speed and the macro-economic criteria favoured by the IMF and the World Bank make it impossible to improve the welfare of the world's poorest peoples. From the point of view of human development, it is a total failure of these two blinkered and overconfident institutions whose well-paid representatives, if they have seen poor people at all, have seen them only on television.

> Modern hi-tech warfare is designed to remove physical contact: dropping bombs from 50,000 feet ensures that one does not 'feel' what one does. Modern economic management is similar: from one's luxury hotel, one can callously impose policies about which one would think twice if one knew the people whose lives one was destroying. *Joseph Stiglitz, Globalization and Its Discontents, 2002*

This failure is not down to bad luck or misunderstanding, but to the deliberate implementation of neo-liberal policies. One might well ask why apparently illogical measures with disastrous consequences for deprived populations are adopted. In fact, structural adjustment makes sense only once it is understood that the IMF seeks above all to serve the interests of finance.

Structural adjustment is composed of two sorts of measures: shock tactics and structural measures. These will be examined in the next two sections.

> Simplistic free market ideology provided the curtain behind which the real business of the 'new' mandate could be transacted. The change in mandate and objectives, while it may have been quiet, was hardly subtle: from serving global economic interests to serving the interests of global finance. Capital market liberalization may not have contributed to global economic stability, but it did open up vast new markets for Wall Street. [...] Looking at the IMF as if it were pursuing the interests of the financial community provides a way of making sense of what might otherwise seem to be contradictory and intellectually incoherent behavior. *Joseph Stiglitz, Globalization and Its Discontents, 2002*

Q15 What are the short-term or shock measures imposed by structural adjustment, and what are their consequences?

1 The imposition of fees for education and healthcare. The IFIs insist on the recovery of costs. Villagers have to contribute to the salaries of the staff in health centres. Pregnant women have to pay for pre-natal consultations – which leads to a rise in perinatal mortality, as a certain number cannot afford to consult. University students have to pay ever-increasing registration fees. Thus, access to higher education is severely limited for young people from the less privileged classes.

2 The end of subsidies on products and services of primary necessity: bread, milk, rice, sugar, fuel.

In the DCs, to compensate for the absence of a guaranteed minimum income, governments traditionally intervene to keep basic foods and other vital goods and services at an affordable price for the poorest sector. The IMF and the World Bank demand that such subsidies be ended. The poorest sections of the population feel the effects immediately. The cost of basic foodstuffs rises and that of fuel, used among other things to prepare the food, goes through the roof. People then have enormous difficulty in cooking food on the one hand, and in boiling water to make it safe to drink on the other, leading to outbreaks of cholera and dysentery. This was what happened in Peru when President Alberto Fujimori implemented a SAP in 1991. Furthermore, public transport costs shoot up, which has immediate repercussions on market-gardening activity. Small farmers who have to bring their produce to market shift the increase on to their sales prices. Fewer daily calories available, inflation of prices, anaemic local economies are major consequences.

There have been numerous cases of rioting following the measures.

- In 1986, in Zambia, the price of foodstuffs increased by 120 per cent, causing hunger riots.
- In 1989, in Venezuela, the SAP caused spectacular increases in the prices of basic products and petrol (and therefore of public transport). In three days of rioting (*el Caracazo*) there were officially 300 deaths (unofficial sources say over 4,000).
- In 1991 in Peru, President Alberto Fujimori applied the orders

of the IMF and the World Bank. The price of petrol increased 31 times and bread 12 times overnight, while the minimum salary fell by over 90 per cent in fifteen years.

- In Jordan, twelve people died in riots in 1989 after the announcement of the rise in the price of fuel imposed by the IMF. In August 1996, further riots broke out in Karakul when bread went up to 2.5 times its price following government subsidy cuts imposed, here again, by the IMF. This did not prevent more subsidy cuts from following on rice, milk and sugar.
- In May 1998, subsidies on basic necessities were cut in Indonesia, causing big riots. In February 2000, following an agreement with the IMF, the Indonesian government raised the price of fuel oil by 30 per cent and of electricity by 20 per cent, with sweeping cuts in the education and health budgets.
- In the Yemen, there were hunger riots in June 1998 after a 40 per cent rise in petroleum prices.
- In August 1999, the Ivory Coast saw riots against a rise in transport fares, following the 17.5 per cent increase in the cost of petroleum products. A young man was killed in Yopougon.
- In Zimbabwe, there were hunger riots in October 2000 when a 30 per cent price-rise on basic necessities such as bread and sugar was announced.
- In 2001 and 2002, Argentina, Paraguay and Uruguay also had rioting and occasional pillaging, often to the sound of saucepans being banged by disgusted housewives.

The list is far from exhaustive.

3 A drastic reduction in public expenditure to balance the budget, particularly by axing social budgets considered 'non-productive' (education, health, housing, infrastructure), by freezing salaries and laying off civil servants.

Of course, this reduction of social budgets directly affects the populations and explains the gravely disturbing human indicators for the DCs mentioned in Q2.

4 Devaluation of local currency.

The main purpose of devaluation (*see* Glossary) is to make local export products cheaper, and thus more competitive on the global market. Theoretically, they are then easier to sell. To earn the same amount of foreign currency, much larger quantities need to be sold. However, the whole idea is nonsensical as several countries practise the same operation at the same time, thus competing with each other. Reciprocally, foreign products become more expensive in those countries. For example, in January 1994, the IMF and France made the African governments of the CFA franc zone devalue that currency by 50 per cent (the CFA franc is the currency used in France's former West African colonies) against the French franc. The effects were disastrous: overnight, a product imported from France that had cost 100 CFA francs cost 200. To earn 100 French francs, you needed to sell twice the amount of merchandise. Thus, the buying power of the populations of the CFA franc zone fell dramatically, all the more so since salaries had been frozen. At the same time, the debts of these countries, in foreign hard currencies, doubled. Twice as much local money was required to buy the amount of foreign currency needed for debt repayments. The effect of devaluation was not the same for all citizens of the affected countries. Poor people saw their buying power halved overnight while the rich, who had been able to make placements abroad in the form of hard currencies, were able, after devaluation, to obtain double the amount in CFA francs for the same amount of hard currency. The local ruling classes knew that devaluation lay ahead and had taken the precaution of changing their CFA francs into foreign hard currency beforehand. This is why it was known as a 'tom-tom devaluation'.

5 High interest rates, to attract foreign capital with a high remuneration.

The trouble is that as the country is in crisis, either the foreign capital does not come in, or it comes in as part of such short-term speculation that it is of no use to the local economy, and in fact may even be harmful as it can lead to an increase in the price of land and housing if the speculation is on the property market. Moreover, small producers borrow on the local market to buy seed, pesticides, weed-killer and so on, and the rise in interest rates radically diminishes their capacity to borrow. Consequently, they sow less and production drops. Firms already in debt have to find extra money for the unexpected repayments just when the market is depressed, leading to numerous bankruptcies. Lastly, the rise in interest rates increases the burden of internal public debt for the state, leading to a worse public deficit when the proclaimed objective was precisely to reduce it. The state then feels obliged to axe social spending even more brutally.

These drastic measures cause many bankruptcies of small and medium-sized firms, as well as national banks. The state finds itself obliged to nationalize them and take over their debts. It reacts by freezing the meagre savings of small-time savers (the '*corralito*' in Argentina). A private debt thus becomes a public one and it is for the tax-payer to take it on. The popular and middle classes are hard hit.

> Brazil has already made so many restrictions in its [public] finances that we don't know what more to restrict, in order to adjust to a world gone mad. *Fernando Henrique Cardoso, President of Brazil, 1 August 2002, cited in Les Echos, 5 August 2002* (trans. VB)

Q16 What are the long-term or structural measures imposed by structural adjustment, and what are their consequences?

1 The development of exports.

To procure the hard currency needed to repay the debt, the DCs need to increase their exports and reduce food crops for the local population (such as manioc or millet, for example). They generally specialize in one (or several) export crops, one (or several) raw materials to be mined, or primary activities such as fishing. They then become highly dependent on this resource or monoculture, as the table overleaf shows.

The economies are all the more unstable because the prices on the global market can suddenly collapse. The great majority of raw materials are exported as such and transformed in the rich countries which then get most of the added value. To simplify, cocoa is produced in Ivory Coast but chocolate is made in France, Belgium and

Country	Principal export product	Share of this product in export revenues for 2000 (%)
Benin	cotton	84
Mali	cotton	47
Burkina Faso	cotton	39
Chad	cotton	38
Uganda	coffee	56
Rwanda	coffee	43
Ethiopia	coffee	40
Nicaragua	coffee	25
Honduras	coffee	22
Tanzania	coffee	20
São Tomé and Príncipe	cocoa	78
Guyana	sugar	25
Malawi	tobacco	61
Mauritania	fishing	54
Senegal	fishing	25
Guinea	bauxite	37
Zambia	copper	48
Niger	uranium	51
Bolivia	natural gas	18
Cameroon	oil	27

Source: IMF, *The Enhanced HIPC Initiative and the Achievement of Long-Term External Debt Sustainability*, 15 April 2002

Switzerland. In Mali, out of the 500,000 tonnes of cotton harvested each year, only 1 per cent is transformed locally.

Finally, to try to increase production, land is often cleared in the forest, with all the ecological consequences of deforestation, especially severe soil erosion and various ill effects on biodiversity.

On a global scale, there are already 1.3 billion people living on fragile land – arid zones, marshy land and forest – from which they cannot get their subsistence. *James Wolfensohn, President of the World Bank, 'Une chance pour le développement durable' [A chance for sustainable development], Le Monde, 23 August 2002* (trans. VB)

2 The opening-up of markets through the elimination of customs barriers.

The official reason for opening up markets is to allow consumers to enjoy lower prices on local markets. However, above all it allows foreign multinationals to conquer considerable market shares in numerous economic sectors, to bring down local producers and, once they have the monopoly, to raise prices on imported products. Locally, inflation and rising unemployment devastate the mass of the population. What use is it to consumers to see the price of beef fall, if having lost their jobs they have no money?

Opening up the markets often leads to foreign production subsidized in the country of origin coming into the local market unhindered and competing freely with local producers, thus destabilizing the local economy. The combat is unequal. Local producers are often less highly trained, less well equipped, and unable to make even modest investments. On the other hand, the multinationals have plentiful means, and the states of the North subsidize their production, especially agricultural, generously. The total amount of subsidies paid by the countries of the North to their agricultural industry is estimated at a billion dollars a day (or over $350 billion a year). Furthermore, the countries of the South are no longer allowed to tax imported goods to protect their own products. This is why, in spite of higher production costs and considerable transport costs, products from the North are often cheaper than the same items produced locally. For example, in 2000, a kilo of home-grown Ivory Coast beef was sold at 1,205 FCFA (about $1.8) in Abidjan, while a kilo of beef imported from the European Union cost 1,035 FCFA ($1.5) because of subsidies. Yet European beef cost 1,740 FCFA ($2.6) a kilo to produce. This happens for all sorts of products throughout the DCs. In summer 2002, chickens imported from the USA cost less on the Dakar market than locally bred chickens, leading to bankruptcy for many Senegalese chicken-farmers.

I am determined to pursue an aggressive strategy of opening up the markets in all the regions of the world. *Bill Clinton, President of the USA, address to the WTO, 18 May 1998*

Let us remember that the developed countries took great care when it was their turn to open up their markets, to do so slowly and methodically, so that it would be carried out under the most favourable conditions. The USA and the other Triad countries protect their industry not only with subsidies but also with protection measures. For example, in 2000, George W. Bush's administration decided to protect the iron and steel industry by applying taxes to steel imported from Europe and Asia. This is exactly what the DCs are prevented from doing!

Is it any surprise, then, with such unfair competition, that the peasant farmers of the Third World cannot manage to feed their families properly, and move to the slums around the big cities in the hope of finding some means of subsistence to replace the living they used to get from their land? How can a local co-operative or small

> Most of the advanced industrial countries – including the USA and Japan – had built up their economies by wisely and selectively protecting some of their industries until they were strong enough to compete with foreign companies. [...] Forcing a developing country to open itself up to imported products that would compete with those produced by certain of its industries, industries that were dangerously vulnerable to competition from much stronger counterpart industries in other countries, can have disastrous consequences – socially and economically. Jobs have systematically been destroyed – poor farmers in developing countries simply could not compete with the highly subsidized goods from Europe and America – before the countries' agricultural and industrial sectors were able to grow strong and create new jobs. Even worse, the IMF's insistence on developing countries maintaining tight monetary policies has led to interest rates that would make job creation impossible even in the best of circumstances. And because trade liberalization occurred before safety-nets were put into place, those who lost their jobs were forced into poverty. Liberalization has thus, too often, not been followed by the promised growth, but by increased misery. *Joseph Stiglitz, Globalization and Its Discontents, 2002*

producer struggling to survive be placed in the same conditions as a multinational from the North? Even the most violent combat sports do not put a featherweight in the ring with a heavyweight, but in the corporate-driven economy, it is 'no holds barred'.

3 The liberalization of the economy, especially the abolition of capital movement control and exchange control.

The idea is to open up the DCs' economies to the investments, products and services of the multinationals of the industrialized countries in order to satisfy the desiderata of the leaders of the multinationals: produce what they like, where they like, in conditions they lay down, at salaries they fix.

Liberalization also aims to eliminate all obstacles preventing the Northern multinationals operating in the DCs from repatriating their profits. As a basis for comparison, in 2001 the profits repatriated by multinationals operating in the DCs were more or less equivalent to the total amount of ODA paid by the countries of the North (sometimes in the form of loans which further increase the debt stock). In other words, the North gives sparingly with one hand what it takes back tenfold with the other. Since we are comparing various financial transfers, note that the ODA is also equivalent to the money saved

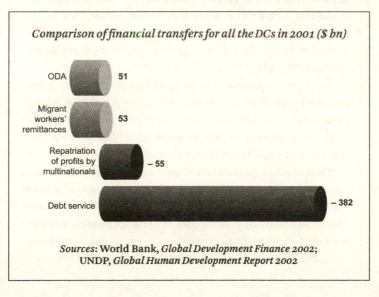

Comparison of financial transfers for all the DCs in 2001 ($ bn)

ODA — 51

Migrant workers' remittances — 53

Repatriation of profits by multinationals — − 55

Debt service — − 382

Sources: World Bank, *Global Development Finance 2002*;
UNDP, *Global Human Development Report 2002*

month by month by migrant workers and sent to their country of origin, which is essential for survival there.

ODA – caution! Official Development Assistance covers numerous financial flows and it is important to relativize the actual amount involved by a precise analysis of its composition. First, ODA consists not only of donations but also of low-interest loans, so in fact part of the ODA increases the debt stock. Furthermore, it is not allocated according to criteria of human development needs; far from it. A large part of aid from the countries of the North is destined above all for their strategic allies. The principal beneficiary of US aid in 2001 was Israel.

Furthermore, not only is aid granted not conditional upon the respect of human rights, but, according to the UNDP (1994), it seems to be systematically directed towards countries with unsatisfactory records in this area: 'In fact, aid paid out by the USA during the 1980s was inversely proportionate to the observance of Human Rights. Multilateral donors do not seem to bother themselves with such considerations, either. Indeed, they seem to prefer authoritarian regimes, maintaining without batting an eyelid that such regimes make for political stability and better economic management. When Bangladesh and the Philippines got rid of martial law, their respective shares of overall World Bank lending fell.'

The same applies to military spending: 'Until 1986, donor countries granted on average five times as much aid per inhabitant to countries with high military spending than to countries which spent less in this field. In 1992, the former were still getting two and a half times as much aid as the latter.'

Thus these geopolitical criteria play a decisive role and can even distort the very notion of aid: 'If aid were directly related to the implementation of certain fundamental human development objectives and to the growing threats against human security in the world, there would be a complete change in how it is distributed. The distribution of ODA would depend on each country's ability to contribute to meeting those objectives. Instead of rationing it out to its favourite clients, ODA would go where the needs were greatest.' In fact, writes the UNDP, the donor countries 'only use an average of 7% of the aid they receive for the most urgent aspects of human development'.

As far as technical aid, supposed to strengthen the DCs' self-sufficiency, is concerned, the situation is no more encouraging: 'It is perhaps even more worrying to observe that after forty years, 90% of the 12 billion dollars spent each year on technical assistance still goes to paying for foreign experts, despite the fact that the beneficiary countries now have their own experts in numerous fields.' The UNDP deplores the fact that 'aid doesn't seem to "take" when institutions and attitudes are in a rut'. For example, 'about a quarter of total annual aid destined for Sub-Saharan Africa is swallowed up financing economists' missions which mostly fail'. What could be clearer!

Debt cancellation is often counted as part of ODA (*see* Q27). Therefore, the share of aid that actually reaches the populations of the DCs is very small. When a country of the North decides to send a plane-load of food and medicines to a country in distress, the cost of chartering the aeroplane, of buying the food and drugs, the salaries of those who prepare or go with the cargo, are all included in the amount of aid that has been given, but the corresponding sums stay in the North. The only thing that may, it is hoped, get to the destination, is the product transported, which usually represents a rather meagre proportion of the sums announced.

Although ODA does not really reach the South, debt service and the profits repatriated by the multinationals actually leave the country. It will be easier to understand the significance of the salaries of migrant workers by looking at the figure on page 61. The money they transfer goes directly to their family back in their home-country.

Sources: UNDP, Global Human Development Report, 1994; Eric Toussaint, Your Money or Your Life, 1998

Lastly, the lifting of all control on capital movements enables the rich of the DCs to delocalize 'their' capital towards the countries of the North instead of investing it in the local economy. The liberalization of capital account transactions therefore causes a haemorrhage of capital (*see* Q44).

In some of the DCs, the ones the international financial institutions (IFIs) call the 'emerging economies', there is another negative consequence. The capital they attract is often very volatile. As soon as there is any sign of economic difficulty, or as soon as another country offers a better deal, the investments are withdrawn, destabilizing the country they flee from. The arrival of such capital caused the speculative bubbles on the stock exchange and in real estate in Southeast Asia in the 1990s. In 1997–98, this volatile capital was brutally withdrawn again, causing a very severe crisis.

> [T]he influx of hot money into and out of the country that so often follows after capital market liberalization leaves havoc in its wake. Small developing countries are like small boats. Rapid capital market liberalization, in the manner pushed by the IMF, amounted to setting them off on a voyage on a rough sea, before the holes in their hulls had been repaired, before the captain had received training, before life vests had been put on board. Even in the best of circumstances, there was a high likelihood that they would be overturned when they were hit broadside by a big wave. *Joseph Stiglitz, Globalization and Its Discontents, 2002*

4 A system of taxation which further aggravates inequalities, with the principle of value-added tax (VAT) and the protection of capital revenues.

The elimination of customs barriers reduces the tax revenues of the state in question, leading to the adoption of a wider taxation system which first and foremost penalizes the poor. The principle of progressive increase is abandoned and VAT generalized. For example, in French-speaking West Africa, VAT is at 18 per cent. It is applied equally to anyone buying a kilo of rice, rich or poor. If someone devotes his entire income to buying staple products to survive, with VAT at 18 per cent, it is as though he were paying 18 per cent extra tax on his entire income – on which he will already have paid income tax at 20–30 per cent. On the other hand, for someone with a high income, of which he uses only, say, 10 per cent for basic products and services, VAT represents only 1.8 per cent of his total income, which in general is taxed at a lower overall rate than wage-earners'. The rest, untaxed, he can invest.

5 Massive privatization of public companies and consequent disengagement of the state from competitive sectors of production.

The enforced privatization of state-owned companies often involves selling them off for a song to the profit of the multinationals of the North and a few well-placed individuals. Money raised through privatization goes straight to repayment of the debt. In Mali, out of ninety public companies in 1985, twenty-six went into liquidation, twenty-eight were privatized and in 2001 there were only thirty-six left. To the IMF, the state has no business doing anything that might make a profit, and should therefore limit its action to repression (police, justice) and withdraw from all other sectors (water, telecommunications, transport, health, education and so on). However, once the railway company, for example, has been privatized, all non-profitable lines are closed down and the population is faced with a reduction in services. This is also accompanied by numerous redundancies, and an increase in unemployment. In Nicaragua, since it veered towards liberalism in 1990, the demands of the IMF have been carried out to the letter, causing 260,000 workers to be laid off in 1994 (out of a total population of less than 4 million inhabitants). The moneyed classes manage but the mass of the population is sinking into poverty and is excluded from a great number of economic activities.

In this way, the state loses control of strategic elements for development. Essential services are entrusted to the private sector, so that there is a blossoming of private educational institutions, often of very mediocre quality, since the requirements in terms of teachers' training and salaries are reduced accordingly.

The agreements signed with the IMF to obtain loans are usually valid for three years. The indebted country commits itself to undertake very specific economic reforms, and the promised sums are handed over in instalments, as these are completed. Thus, in Madagascar, the privatization of the state-owned petroleum company (Solima) fell behind the timetable planned by the IMF. Planned for 1999, it was not completed until June 2000. In July 2000, the first instalment of a new loan was paid, as a reward for being good. Result: a company sold off cut-price into private ownership and an increase in the country's indebtedness. For the population: nothing.

All in all, structural adjustment programmes defend the interests of the financial institutions and the multinationals of the North. But for the populations who have to bear their consequences, they are synonymous with poverty and hardship.

> As economics is not an exact science, the number of counter-examples is irrelevant. If I put forward a hypothesis in physics which is proved wrong by an experiment, I must question the theory. And the theory progresses through such invalidation. In economics, you can undermine the existence of millions of people, but none of that human evidence will affect the ideology of structural adjustment. *Susan George, Vice-President of ATTAC France, in Charlie Hebdo, 6 December 2000* (trans. VB)

Q17 What is the role of the Paris Club?

The Paris Club is the name given to the group formed by nineteen creditor states (Western Europe, Canada, USA, Japan, Australia, Russia), which meet about once a month at the French Ministry of Finance at Bercy (Paris), to make sure the indebted states keep up their repayments on their bilateral external public debt. These sessions of what are called 'negotiations' always deal with countries one at a time, under the attentive eye of the multilateral institutions. In official terms, the Club's role is to 'negotiate' the 'right solution' with countries in difficulty. Its objective is clear: to bring the maximum amount of money into the coffers of the creditor states of the North, and to prevent the debtor states from getting into the habit of deferring payments, suspending them or, worst of all, cancelling them.

The Paris Club, as will have been understood, does not in any way act as a development agency, but mainly as a debt-recovery agency. It observes a situation which it deems purely financial with a cold and implacable gaze. The Paris Club itself says this quite clearly on its website: 'The creditors of the Paris Club wish to recover the maximum of their debts. Thus they demand immediate payment of the highest amount possible.'

The Paris Club presents itself as an informal group, a 'non-institution'. It has neither legal existence nor statutes. The results of its activities, transcribed in the approved minutes at the end of each session, are not binding for the creditor states; they are simply recommendations, but the creditor states undertake to implement them and it is at this point that they acquire legal value. In other words, the Paris Club, which conducts all the analyses and negotiations and incites the creditor countries to make decisions with grave consequences for the debtor countries who stand before them, does not actually exist. This is a very practical way to avoid being taken to court and having to be accountable.

Yet the Club plays a fundamental role in allowing the states of the North to present a united front for debt-recovery, while each debtor country is necessarily isolated, in a very uncomfortable position. In short, the negotiations are rigged.

As judge in its own case, the Paris Club is anything but democratic on the inside and opaque from the outside. It is rarely possible to learn what was said in the internal discussions at each session. However, the Club's logic is perfectly clear. It is part of the policy of debt-management imposed by the IMF and the World Bank. A country can go before the Paris Club to ask to have its debt rescheduled only after it has signed an agreement with the IMF. This means that the IMF also controls the rescheduling of bilateral debts by the Paris Club, whose aim is to delay repayments by deciding on some years of grace (i.e. the years when there will not be any repayment), or by spreading them over longer periods. Clearly, the Paris Club negotiates only with countries that are already under the IMF's thumb.

Moreover, to discover whether a country is genuinely having difficulty in meeting the payments, a study of the country's financial capacities is carried out. This appraisal is based on IMF forecasts and conclusions, which are often far removed from reality. In the case of Mali, in 2000, the IMF forecast an increase in volume of exports of 9 per cent a year over five years whereas, in 2001, the price of cotton, Mali's main exportable commodity, fell by 40 per cent on the global market. There are dozens of such examples of erroneous forecasts. It is more the general rule than the exception.

The first time a country presents itself, the Paris Club fixes on a date. Officially, only loans made before that date are affected by the rescheduling. Debts contracted after the date do not usually qualify for restructuring. This is so as to reassure the financial markets and the money-lenders that any new loans granted will be repaid. For Madagascar, Niger or Ivory Coast, the date was 1 July 1983, which considerably reduces the volume of debt concerned.

The Paris Club distinguishes between two kinds of debt: ODA loans granted at lower interest rates than those of the market, which are supposed to enhance development,[1] and non-ODA loans (or commercial loans), which are the only ones which may qualify for reduction.

Generally, debt-reduction by the Paris Club is reserved for the poorest and the most heavily indebted countries. Of course, there are exceptions to this rule when it happens to be a country of strategic importance (this is the case for Russia; see page 69). On the whole, for the great majority of DCs with payment difficulties, the Paris Club responds with debt-rescheduling, which merely postpones the problem to a later date.

For example, after its programme had been approved by the IMF on 19 December 2000, the Ukraine went before the Paris Club for the first time on 13 July 2001. Arrears at this date plus the instalments due from then until the end of 2002 came to $770 million. Of this sum, the Paris Club rescheduled 578 million, to be repaid in eighteen instalments between 2005 and 2013.

Thus, every month, states whose economies are under the strict control of the IMF go before the Paris Club to postpone repayment

---

1 In principle; but more and more often these ODA credits are destined to support structural adjustment programmes that prevent any real development. They generally maintain existing poverty when they do not actually create it.

Russia's moratorium went unsanctioned

Certain grandiloquent declarations by the Paris Club are quite simply contradicted by the facts. In 1998, Russia decreed a unilateral moratorium and has received absolutely no sanctions. On the contrary, it has greatly benefited from the unilateral suspension of payments. What is going on?

Faced with a fall in its export revenues (a fall in the price of oil in 1998) and tax revenues, Russia unilaterally suspended debt repayments for three months, starting from August 1998. This enabled it to modify the power balance in its favour, with regard to its Paris Club and London Club creditors. Thanks to the suspension, it obtained the cancellation of about 30 per cent of its debt towards these two categories of creditors. Its status as a former nuclear superpower no doubt helped it to force the negotiations through.

As for the IMF, it has continued to grant loans to Russia despite the suspension (i.e. in contradiction of its own declarations) while several billion dollars have been embezzled via Western European tax havens by top Russian officials converted to capitalism.

We have no sympathy for the Russian leaders who are conducting a ruthless war against the Chechen people and who are applying anti-social and corporate-driven policies throughout the whole of Russia. However, there is a lesson to be learnt from this suspension of payment: an openly defiant attitude to the creditors can pay off (*see* Q30).

of certain loans for several years, or even one or two decades. What a poisoned chalice to hand to future generations!

There is a very clear form of blackmail to dissuade indebted countries from forming a 'front of refusal'. It can be read on the Paris Club website <www.clubdeparis.org>:

The quality of a financial signature is built up in the long term in so far as lenders tend to judge the capacity of a borrower to repay his debts over a long period, before according him further funds. On the other hand, the financial signature of a country can lose status rapidly if contractual obligations are not met. When debt rescheduling proves unavoidable, countries which do not accumulate arrears and which adopt preventive measures to find a solution in co-operation with the creditors, particularly within the Paris Club, will be able to win back their borrowing facilities more easily. However, those which declare a unilateral moratorium tend to lose the chance of obtaining further funding for a time.

Finally, it is important to note that, after going before the Paris Club, the indebted state can then turn to its private bank creditors, grouped in the London Club. Here the negotiations are of a similar type, but even more opaque and with an even worse stink of profit at all costs.

Today, the emerging markets are not forced open under the threat of the use of military might, but through economic power, through the threat of sanctions or the withholding of needed assistance in a time of crisis. *Joseph Stiglitz, Globalization and Its Discontents, 2002*

Q18 Are all the DCs in the same boat?

Yes and no.

In the first instance, it is tempting to answer yes. Practically all the DCs have been laid low by the debt crisis. For most, the IMF and the World Bank imposed uniform structural adjustment programmes, with all the ensuing negative consequences enumerated in Q15 and Q16, without considering two essential factors:

- the opinions of the populations, who were never consulted, even though it is they who are primarily concerned
- the specific characteristics of each country, which often have fundamentally different assets

There is indeed no doubt that the 165 DCs have different histo-

It is true that there was a tendency at the IMF, about ten years ago, to think that there was a universal answer. That a development model that had worked well in one part of the world could be transposed, just as it was, anywhere else. This gave rise to programmes which paid too little attention to the concrete consequences for the populations of the countries concerned. It has to be said, they were worked out by technocrats – often American – who, it seemed, could not care less about the local consequences of their plans. *Philippe Maystadt, former President of the Interim Committee of the IMF* (trans. VB)

ries and different assets. How can the advanced economies of Brazil, Mexico, India or South Korea be compared with those of Bangladesh or the poorest countries of Sub-Saharan Africa? Each underwent the debt crisis in its own way, struggling as best it could, but each went under.

Latin America served as a laboratory for ultra-liberalism. From the 1980s onwards, very harsh measures were planned and applied there, before being generalized indiscriminately throughout the rest of the world. The crises of 1982 and 1994 in Mexico, 1998–99 in Brazil, 2001 in Argentina, 2002 in Brazil, Uruguay and the whole region, have profoundly shaken the continent, with lasting consequences.

The East Asian Tigers (Indonesia, Thailand, Malaysia, the Philippines) managed to attain strong economic positions which gave them a certain amount of room to manoeuvre until the mid-1990s. However, the 1997 crisis forced them under, later but just as brutally. Malaysia refused any agreement with the IMF in 1997–98, protected its domestic market and, after the crisis had broken out, took strict control of capital flows and exchange, and the government spent money on giving new impetus to production. Whereas the IMF announced impending disaster, Malaysia was back on its feet before the other countries affected.

Sub-Saharan Africa's decolonization in the 1960s meant the withdrawal of the former colonial powers. Those countries did not have the economic arms to hold out for long. A large number fell prey to the IMF and the World Bank, who began to pilot their economies very early on, effectively replacing former colonial exploitation with the debt burden.

Certain East European countries became heavily indebted from the end of the 1970s. In the early 1990s, after the collapse of the former Soviet Union and the fall of the Berlin Wall, all those countries were rapidly delivered up to the ferocious appetites of accelerated liberalization, and social conditions fast deteriorated. The 1998 crisis in Russia hastened the country's decline, with life expectancy falling by about four years during the 1990s, while industrial production fell by 60 per cent and the GDP by 54 per cent.

Just these few examples show how submission to the debt mechanism can differ from one country to the next. This submission was further facilitated by the corruption of the ruling classes of the DCs, who soon learnt how to cash in on their docility regarding the international financial institutions, of whom the least that can be said is that they were willing accomplices.

Sometimes, however, certain especially selected countries have apparently benefited from favouritism. Countries in this case are strategic allies, useful at the time for the geopolitical interests of the powers of the North. Usually, they negotiate their support in exchange for new loans and debt-rescheduling, or even some debt-reduction. These measures, however loudly trumpeted in the media, have never actually involved massive debt-cancellation. They have mainly been used to sweeten the local populations and get them to accept unwelcome alliances. Some examples follow.

In April 1991, Poland went before the Paris Club which had decided to reschedule all debts owing to its members, i.e. almost $30 billion. Thus was Poland rewarded for opening up to liberalization, as the first East European state to join the Western camp by leaving the Warsaw Pact (*see* Glossary). Nevertheless, despite the promises, Poland was to see its bilateral public debt service increase from $183 million in 1991, to $353 million in 1992, to $755 million in 1993. This led the Polish President, Lech Walesa, to protest that his country had been very poorly rewarded indeed.

In May 1991, Egypt's bilateral debt up to $21 billion was rescheduled, to thank it for its co-operation during the Gulf War against Iraq.

The service on the bilateral public debt was thus divided by two: from $1,100 million in 1990, to $550 million in 1991, before climbing back to $800 million in 1992 and 1993. But its bilateral public debt continues to increase.

In November 2001, the former Yugoslavia benefited from generous treatment for the whole of its debt on behalf of the Paris Club, which granted it the conditions normally reserved for the poorest countries. This favour came after the new Serb government had handed the former leader, Slobodan Milosevic, over to the International Criminal Tribunal in The Hague on 29 June 2001.

In December 2001, Pakistan was thanked for having broken with the Afghan Taliban and for forming an alliance with the USA during its operations in Afghanistan after the 11 September attacks. The Paris Club advantageously restructured almost the entire debt owed to it by Islamabad.

These few cases show the extent to which debt-management is linked to geopolitical imperatives, at a given time. The states of the North use the debt as a means of domination over the DCs. As soon as it is in their interests, as soon as they have the political will to win over a temporary ally, they know how to manipulate debt-reduction or cancellation as a lever to reach their ends.

> Your Reporter notes that conditionality often means imposing a pre-established line of conduct upon the country benefiting from the IMF's intervention. This conduct is rarely adapted to the reality of their economic and social structures, but is modelled on the developed economies which, let it be remembered, have only reached their present stage of development after decades, even centuries, of economic evolution. *Yves Tavernier, French MP, French National Assembly's Finance Commission's Report on the Activities and Control of the IMF and the World Bank, 2001* (trans. VB)

FIVE

Anatomy of the developing countries' debt

Q19 What does the external debt of the DCs consist of?

We shall try to analyse the structure of the DCs' external debt using round figures for simplicity's sake.

In 2001, the total external debt of the DCs was estimated at about $2,450 billion.

From the creditors' point of view, the multilateral portion comes to $450 billion, the bilateral portion to $500 billion and the private portion to $1,500 billion:

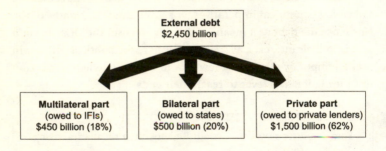

From the debtors' point of view, the distribution is as follows:

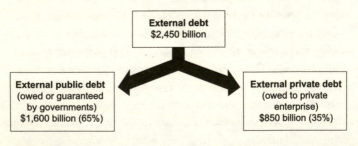

The geographical distribution of the external debt of the DC can be seen on Map 2 (*see* page xii).

The most industrialized DCs are also the most indebted (see overleaf).

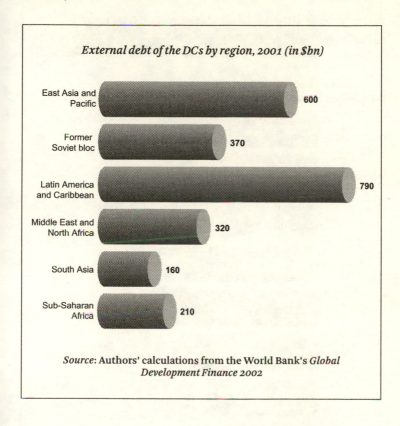

External debt of the DCs by region, 2001 (in $bn)

East Asia and Pacific	600
Former Soviet bloc	370
Latin America and Caribbean	790
Middle East and North Africa	320
South Asia	160
Sub-Saharan Africa	210

Source: Authors' calculations from the World Bank's *Global Development Finance 2002*

Q20 Who are the main creditors of the different DCs?

For the DCs taken as a whole, the private part of the debt is the greatest, ahead of the bilateral and multilateral parts (*see* Q19).

However, from one country to another, there are fairly significant disparities. Countries with strategic raw materials or with a good level of industrialization can guarantee their repayments. Private financial institutions (banks, pension funds [*see* Glossary], insurance companies, mutual funds [*see* Glossary]) are therefore happy to make loans and the major portion of the debt of these countries is private. This is the case for countries such as Brazil, Argentina, Chile, Venezuela,

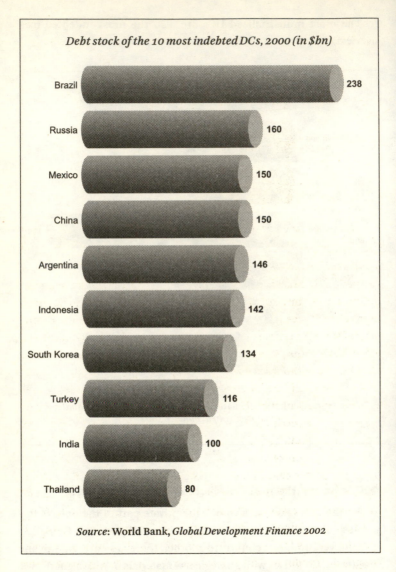

Debt stock of the 10 most indebted DCs, 2000 (in $bn)

Brazil	238
Russia	160
Mexico	150
China	150
Argentina	146
Indonesia	142
South Korea	134
Turkey	116
India	100
Thailand	80

Source: World Bank, *Global Development Finance 2002*

Mexico, South Africa, South Korea, Malaysia, Turkey, Hungary, the Czech Republic, Slovakia or Croatia.

Certain very poor countries which nevertheless have mineral resources also receive loans from private financial institutions. This is the case for Angola, Congo-Brazzaville and Nigeria.

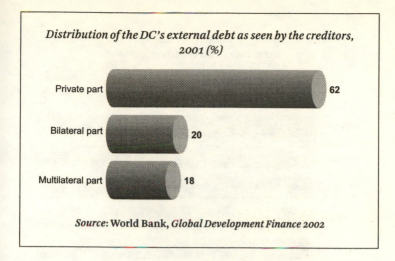

Distribution of the DC's external debt as seen by the creditors, 2001 (%)

Private part — 62
Bilateral part — 20
Multilateral part — 18

Source: World Bank, *Global Development Finance 2002*

On the other hand, private banks and other private financial institutions are not interested in the poorest countries which do not have mineral resources. They have withdrawn from them since the beginning of the debt crisis in the 1980s. Since then, they have refused to make fresh loans. In a word, the banks are collecting repayments of old debts without granting new ones (or else, in the short term, with extra-high interest rates). The IMF and the World Bank as well as governments of the industrialized countries have lent money to the poorest countries to enable them to repay the banks. The IMF and the World Bank have reached the point where they are by far the principal creditors of some of the most indebted countries. Thus they hold over 80 per cent of the debts of Burkina Faso, Burundi, Chad, Gambia, Malawi, Uganda, Haiti and Nepal. The huge debt burden of these countries confers total power on the lending institutions.

In other indebted countries, states of the North share this role with the IFIs, as for example in Mauritania, Mali, Ethiopia, Guinea, Guyana or Honduras. This is because, very often, a large part of the bilateral debt is money owed to private firms of the countries making the loans. The firms obtain coverage from their governments, particularly through export credit agencies (*see* Glossary), such as Coface in France or Ducroire in Belgium.

The following chart illustrates the different debt structures.

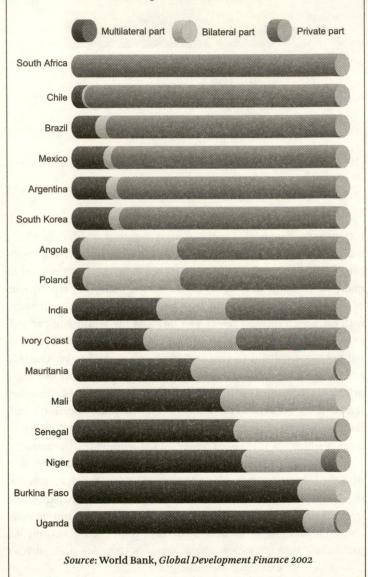

Distribution of long-term external debt of the different DCs according to the creditors, 2000

Multilateral part   Bilateral part   Private part

South Africa
Chile
Brazil
Mexico
Argentina
South Korea
Angola
Poland
India
Ivory Coast
Mauritania
Mali
Senegal
Niger
Burkina Faso
Uganda

Source: World Bank, *Global Development Finance 2002*

Q21 How have the roles of the different creditors evolved over the last thirty years?

A first glance shows that the debt burden in each of the six regions of DCs has greatly increased over the last thirty years.

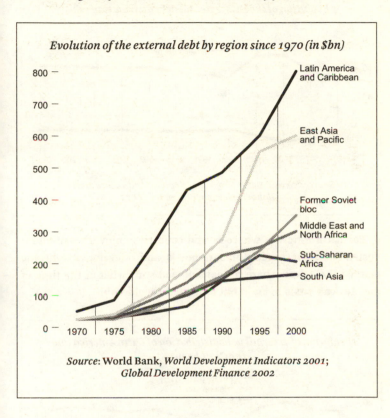

Evolution of the external debt by region since 1970 (in $bn)

Latin America and Caribbean

East Asia and Pacific

Former Soviet bloc

Middle East and North Africa

Sub-Saharan Africa

South Asia

Source: World Bank, *World Development Indicators 2001*;
Global Development Finance 2002

Now let us look at how it pans out per creditor from 1970 until the present. There is a lot to be learned from this. From 1970 until 1980, as we have seen, the four actors in the increase of indebtedness were private banks, the states of the North, the World Bank and the governments of the South. Of these the most active were the private banks of the Northern states; the private part of the debt was predominant. Following the sudden rise in interest rates in 1979, and the ensuing debt crisis, private banks began to disengage from countries without strategic resources or successful industries, such as Sub-Saharan

Africa, in favour of places where profits were higher (especially Latin America and Asia). Below are figures for the DCs overall.

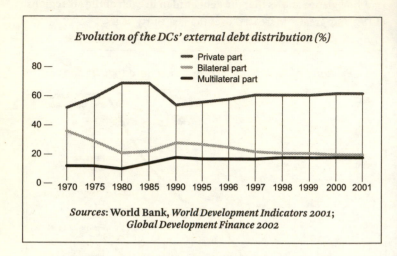

Evolution of the DCs' external debt distribution (%)

Sources: World Bank, *World Development Indicators 2001*; *Global Development Finance 2002*

For Latin America, where several countries enjoy diversified industry, natural resources (oil or minerals) and a developed domestic market, the private share of loans dipped somewhat at the time of the Mexican crisis in 1994 but remained considerable.

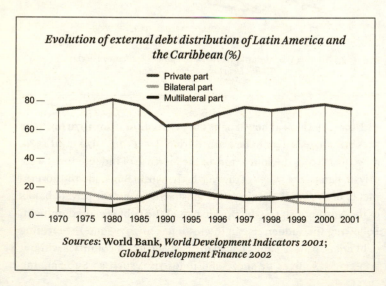

Evolution of external debt distribution of Latin America and the Caribbean (%)

Sources: World Bank, *World Development Indicators 2001*; *Global Development Finance 2002*

East Asia shows more or less the same profile, with a fall in the private share of the debt following the crisis of 1997.

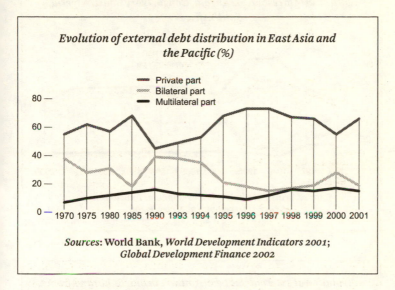

Evolution of external debt distribution in East Asia and the Pacific (%)

Sources: World Bank, *World Development Indicators 2001*; *Global Development Finance 2002*

The profile for Sub-Saharan African countries varies a lot according to whether or not the country concerned has strategic resources. For countries such as Angola, Congo, Nigeria or South Africa, which have oil, gold or diamonds, and for Ivory Coast (a major exporter of cocoa and coffee), the private part of the external debt dropped in the 1980s but remains fairly high (see page 82).

Note the increase in the bilateral share from 1985 on, to the detriment of the private share. For 2000, the variations are due to the doubling of the bilateral share for Nigeria alone (from $13 billion to $26 billion). In 2002, that country had severe repayment difficulties mainly because creditors refused to grant debt reduction, just when oil revenues fell.

On the other hand, for countries less well endowed with desirable resources, the private part of the debt is small, and the multilateral share grows as the years go by.

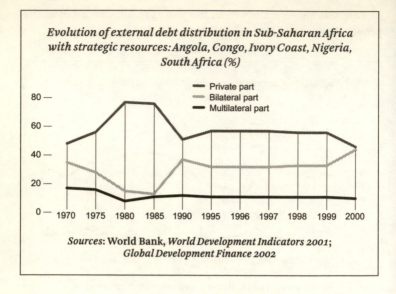

Evolution of external debt distribution in Sub-Saharan Africa with strategic resources: Angola, Congo, Ivory Coast, Nigeria, South Africa (%)

Sources: World Bank, *World Development Indicators 2001*;
Global Development Finance 2002

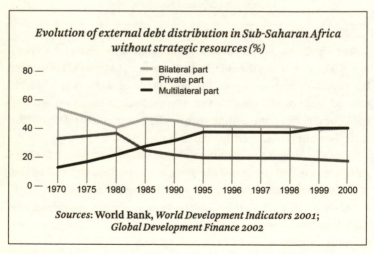

Evolution of external debt distribution in Sub-Saharan Africa without strategic resources (%)

Sources: World Bank, *World Development Indicators 2001*;
Global Development Finance 2002

Q22 Do the DCs repay their debts?

Although major economic problems sometimes prevent some DCs from continuing their repayments over limited periods, the immense majority honour their financial commitments. Thus the total

amount paid in debt-servicing for 2001 came to $382 billion (*see* Map 4, page xiv), distributed over the six DC regions as follows:

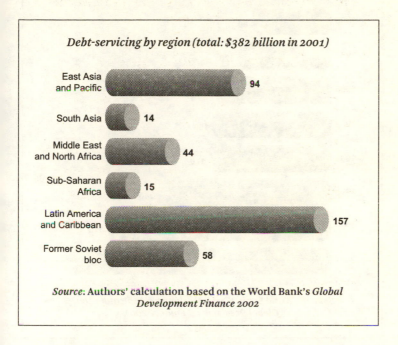

Debt-servicing by region (total: $382 billion in 2001)

East Asia and Pacific	94
South Asia	14
Middle East and North Africa	44
Sub-Saharan Africa	15
Latin America and Caribbean	157
Former Soviet bloc	58

Source: Authors' calculation based on the World Bank's *Global Development Finance 2002*

It should not be imagined that 2001 was in any way an exception. If we study debt-servicing payments over the period 1980–2001, we note a steady increase. From $90 billion in 1980, $160 billion in 1990 and $240 billion in 1995, they reached $382 billion in 2001 (see page 84, top).

Total repayments between 1980 and 2001 came to about $4,500 billion.

What does the bottom chart on page 84 show? It reveals that for every $1 owed in 1980, the DCs have repaid $7.50 but still owe $4.

The amounts to be repaid are so enormous that fresh loans have to be taken out to repay the original ones. Following this logic, the debt will be perpetuated indefinitely, as will the highly subtle tool of domination that it represents.

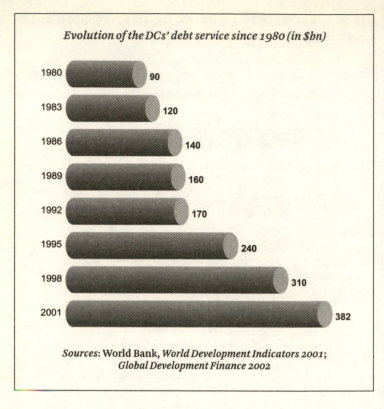

Evolution of the DCs' debt service since 1980 (in $bn)

1980	90
1983	120
1986	140
1989	160
1992	170
1995	240
1998	310
2001	382

Sources: World Bank, *World Development Indicators 2001*;
Global Development Finance 2002

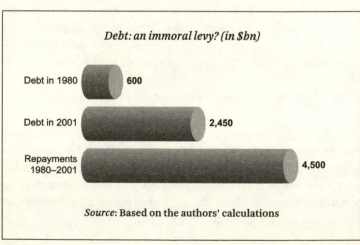

Debt: an immoral levy? (in $bn)

Debt in 1980	600
Debt in 2001	2,450
Repayments 1980–2001	4,500

Source: Based on the authors' calculations

Q23 How are the debt-related financial flows managed?

The generous-sounding declarations of the rich countries about the so-called aid they claim to provide may lead us to wonder whether the DCs receive more in new loans than they repay to service their debts. In other words, does the flow of money related to the debt run from North to South or from South to North?

The answer is stark: financial flows are strongly negative for the countries of the South, which means that the DCs transfer wealth to the North, and not the reverse. Given below are the figures for the net transfer (*see* Glossary) concerning the debt by region for 2001. All are negative, indicating that the financial flows leave the DCs.

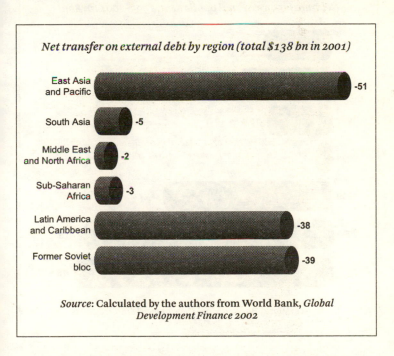

Net transfer on external debt by region (total $138 bn in 2001)

East Asia and Pacific -51
South Asia -5
Middle East and North Africa -2
Sub-Saharan Africa -3
Latin America and Caribbean -38
Former Soviet bloc -39

Source: Calculated by the authors from World Bank, *Global Development Finance 2002*

This is what is known as the 'vicious debt spiral'. The DCs have had to take out fresh loans in order to make such repayments. What has actually happened is that since the mid-1980s, transfers have changed direction and now go systematically from the South to the North.

Examining the impact of the Southeast Asian and Latin American crises region by region since 1998 could not be more eloquent. In all, no fewer than $440 billion were transferred from the DCs to the Triad (*see* Map 3 on page xiii).

Now let us examine net transfers relating to the external public debt more closely. Here, too, the states of the South or the organizations whose debts they guarantee have transferred gigantic sums to the North. Between 1995 and 2001, the DCs paid out $248 billion more than they received in new loans.

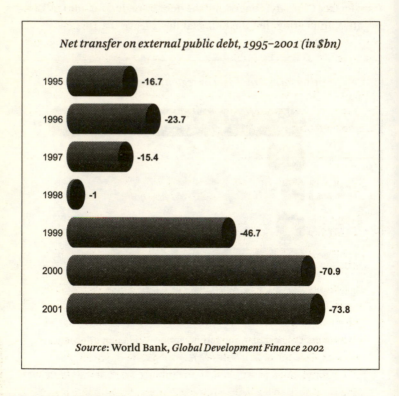

Net transfer on external public debt, 1995–2001 (in $bn)

1995	-16.7
1996	-23.7
1997	-15.4
1998	-1
1999	-46.7
2000	-70.9
2001	-73.8

Source: World Bank, *Global Development Finance 2002*

The low figure for 1998 is due to the considerable loans granted during the Asian crisis, which spread to Russia and Brazil. That year, the massive arrival of funds collected by the IMF to save debtors and creditors from bankruptcy restored the balance of net transfers related to the debt without, however, reversing the tendency. In the following years, since the debt had significantly increased, repayments also increased, accentuating the transfer of wealth from the DCs to their creditors in the North.

Yet these figures still need to be added to, for a true estimate of real flows. As well as repayments on the external debt, we have to include capital outflow due to the wealthy of the DCs; repatriation of profits by multinationals (including invisible transfers, especially using methods of 'over-' or 'under-charging'); acquisition of DCs' businesses at rock-bottom prices by the dominant classes of the industrialized countries, within a framework of privatization policies; low-cost purchase of basic goods produced by the DCs' populations (with deteriorating exchange rates); the 'brain drain'; theft of genetic resources. The donors are not what they would have us believe.

To summarize, the debt is a powerful mechanism for the transfer of wealth from small producers in the South to the capital-holders in the North, with the dominant classes of the DCs skimming off their commission on the way.

The DCs sent fifty-six Marshall Plans to their creditors between 1980 and 2001

At the end of the Second World War, the Marshall Plan for the reconstruction of Europe, financed by the USA, cost about $12.5 billion at the time, i.e. less than $80 billion at today's value. Thus, in repaying $4,500 billion, the populations of the DCs have sent to their creditors in the North the equivalent of fifty-six Marshall Plans, from which the local capitalist elite have taken their commissions. Part of this comes back to the South in the form of new loans to ensure that the transfers continue. From a mathematical point of view, the debt is self-perpetuating. The financial pillage of the populations of the South by the ruling classes of the North, aided and abetted by their Southern counterparts, is taking place under our very eyes.

SIX

Ongoing moves to reduce the debt burden

Q24 How did the debt-reduction initiative come about?

Creditors do not usually cancel debts, and even more rarely do they give presents. Yet in the press, we regularly read about debt-reduction and cancellation. What is going on?

Since the G7 summit in Toronto in 1988, the debt has been recognized as a structural problem. The rich states subsequently tried to organize rescheduling of debt payments and a few meagre reduction measures for the many countries that were accumulating payment arrears and trying to persuade their creditors to postpone the deadlines. These measures have invariably proved insufficient and inappropriate, leaving the debt problem intact.

As for the multilateral part, the IMF and World Bank statutes forbid them to cancel debts. This provides a handy justification for systematic refusal. Until 1996, only bilateral and private debt reductions were discussed.

The Paris Club, which manages bilateral reductions conceded by its member countries, plays a decisive role in this respect. The measures it decides upon often serve as a basis for agreements with bilateral creditors not belonging to the Paris Club and with private creditors, on the principle of comparable treatment. We have seen that the Paris Club sometimes grants reduction of part of the debt, and rescheduling of the rest. Over the years and the G7 summits, the percentage to be reduced has had to be revised upwards, since it was still not sufficient to enable the countries concerned to escape from the spiral of postponed repayments. Crises came faster and thicker. The percentage, originally fixed at 33 per cent in Toronto in 1988, was raised to 50 per cent in London in 1991 then to 67 per cent in Naples in 1994.

Even the few highly mediatized debt-reduction announcements we have heard about since 1990 are very disappointing. Reductions have been reserved for strategic allies of the USA or the four other big powers (Japan, Germany, France, the United Kingdom). Those who have benefited have been, among others, Poland (to encourage it to leave the Warsaw Pact), Egypt (for support during the first Gulf War against Iraq), or more recently Pakistan (for support during the war in Afghanistan) and Yugoslavia (to persuade it to hand over Slobodan Milosevic). In any case, the total amount turned out to be very limited. No doubt the populations of these countries, none too enthusiastic about enrolling politically or economically under the US 'star-spangled banner', had to be persuaded.

Meanwhile, another big power has cancelled debts, though with scant attention from the media. Russia, in the 1990s, renounced a large part of the money it was owed by Nicaragua, Mozambique, Vietnam, and so on, which did not prevent it from benefiting from a considerable debt-reduction itself (*see* box in Q17, page 69).

In 1996, faced with the ballooning debt crisis, the world's great money-spinners came up with a new debt-reduction initiative, which is still in effect, highly mediatized and not without ulterior motives. It is the HIPC initiative.

> Must we really let our children die of hunger to repay our debts?
> *Julius Nyerere, President of Tanzania, 1964–85*

Q25 What is the Heavily Indebted Poor Countries (HIPC) initiative?

The HIPC initiative, launched at the G7 summit in Lyon in 1996 and consolidated at that of Cologne in September 1999, is supposed to reduce the debts of poor, heavily indebted countries. But it got off on the wrong foot, and has solved nothing. It concerns only a small number of very poor countries (42 out of 165 DCs) (*see* Appendix) and its aim goes no further than to make the external debt sustainable. The IMF and the World Bank are trying to reduce the debt just enough to keep debtors out of arrears and to end requests for rescheduling. Nothing more! As we shall see, they have not even reached this goal. Worse still, they take advantage of this apparently generous initiative to impose ever stricter structural adjustment. Behind the illusion of change, the same old logic continues, undeterred.

Compared to previous debt-reduction initiatives, note that, for the first time, this one concerns all the creditors, even the multilateral institutions. The special procedure that brought this about will be described in detail later. As we shall see, it is a procedure that involves the institutions as little as possible in the reductions but as much as possible in decision-making.

To benefit from debt-reduction within the HIPC initiative framework, a country must go through numerous demanding stages that all take an inordinately long time.

First of all, countries hoping to qualify must, according to the IMF, 'be indebted to an intolerable degree', and 'establish positive antecedents in implementing reforms and good economic policies through programmes supported by the World Bank and the IMF'. It is a real obstacle race. A country concerned by the initiative must first sign an agreement with the IMF whereby for three years it will carry out an economic policy approved by Washington. This policy is based on drawing up a Poverty Reduction Strategy Paper (PRSP; *see* Glossary). This document, which takes some time to produce, plays an interim role to begin with. It presents the economic situation of the country and has to give a detailed list of privatizations and economic deregulation measures that can generate resources to repay the debt. It also has to set out how funds resulting from debt-reduction will be used, particularly to combat poverty. The contradiction is clear. Officially, the PRSP is to be drawn up within a vast process of democratic participation, in collaboration with local civil society.

At the end of the three-year period, the IMF and the World Bank try to find out whether the policy adopted by the country is sufficient to enable it to repay its debt. The criterion for determining whether the debt is unsustainable is the ratio between the present value of the debt and the annual amount of export revenue. If the ratio exceeds 150 per cent, the debt is judged unsustainable.[1] In this case, the

---

1 To give the complete picture, we should mention that certain very poor countries are particularly open and have a high amount of annual exports. Despite being heavily over-indebted, their debt might be considered as sus-

country has reached the decision point and is declared to qualify for the HIPC initiative.

It then benefits from some preliminary reductions (known as 'intermediary'), which affect the service of the debt only for the period covered by the agreement with the IMF. These reductions can reach 90 per cent since the Cologne G7 summit. But let there be no mistake: at this stage the debt stock of the country concerned has not diminished; simply, the amounts of certain repayments have been reduced.

A country that successfully reaches the decision point must then pursue its implementation of policies approved by the IMF and draw up a final PRSP. This can take between one and three years, determined by completion of the document and the satisfactory setting up of the key reforms agreed with the IMF. These key reforms correspond in fact to reinforcement of the structural adjustment of the 1980s and 1990s, renamed PRSP for the circumstance.

Then comes the completion point. The country's bilateral debt stock is then cancelled, in accordance with the terms of Cologne. Officially, this means 90 per cent of non-ODA debt stock before the deadline. In reality, it is often difficult to verify. The repayments on the multilateral part of the debt are reduced, without any actual cancellation, so that the country can get back to a situation of sustainable overall debt by IMF criteria.

Let us take the example of Tanzania. In November 1996, it signed a structural adjustment programme approved by the IMF. On 5 April 2000, a little over three years after its agreement with the IMF, it had reached the decision point in the HIPC initiative. After 14 April 2000, it was back at the Paris Club, which agreed to take into account $711 million, which was more or less what the debt service over the following three years would be, in the terms of the

---

tainable. For these countries to benefit from the initiative, another criterion was added. Countries with an exports-to-GDP ratio of more than 30 per cent and a budget revenue-to-GDP ratio of more than 15 per cent (to ensure that the level of revenue brought into play is satisfactory), the criterion selected for a debt to be deemed unsustainable is a ratio of the present value of the debt over budget revenue of over 250 per cent. This is the criterion that allowed countries like Ivory Coast or Guyana to be declared eligible for the HIPC initiative.

Cologne agreement. Once the completion point was reached on 27 November 2001, Tanzania went back to the Paris Club in January 2002. Its total external debt was about $7.5 billion, of which 2.9 billion was the bilateral part. The IMF and the World Bank soon announced $3 billion of reduction on the debt service. It was pure trickery, as those $3 billion represented a remission on repayments of about $100 million a year for thirty years! Meanwhile, fresh debts will have been amassed and, because of neo-liberal measures, export revenues will have fallen again and millions of people will have died of easily treatable diseases or of malnutrition.

> The complete implementation of the initiative will not result in a reduction in value [...] of the debt, as the reductions will mainly take the form of remissions of interest payments and donations destined to finance debt servicing, and not direct reductions of the debt stock. *OECD, External Debt Statistics, 1998–99*

Concerning the so-called reductions of the multilateral part of the debt, a fund called the HIPC Trust Fund has been set up. It is run by the IDA (*see* Q13). The rich countries and multilateral institutions are encouraged to contribute to this fund. The sums received are placed on the financial markets, and thus contribute to swelling the speculation bubble. The profits are destined to finance the reductions. The multilateral institutions, which have decided not to cancel anything, even though they can afford to, repay themselves from this kitty. So whether the repayments come from the Trust Fund or from the DC, it makes no difference to the IMF and the World Bank. To speak of debt cancellation in these circumstances is a deliberate abuse of language, which makes them look good. One thing is quite clear: there is no multilateral debt cancellation.

Altogether, there are forty-two HIPCs, of which thirty-four are in Sub-Saharan Africa, four in Latin America (Honduras, Nicaragua, Bolivia, Guyana), three in Asia (Laos, Vietnam and Myanmar) and Yemen. However, they will not all get reductions. Indeed, Laos has not applied for the initiative, as its leaders consider that the disadvantages far outweigh the advantages. Then there are four countries that reached the decision point only to get a negative answer: Angola, Kenya, Vietnam and Yemen. Their debt burden is judged sustainable, even though Angola, for example, devastated by twenty-five years of civil war fostered by the oil multinationals, had to face an unprecedented famine in 2000. Forecasts indicate that a further three countries will not qualify for the initiative (because of a state of war or lack of co-operation with the rich countries). They are Liberia, Sudan and Somalia, thus sanctioned for not being politically correct. So the HIPC initiative concerns at best thirty-four countries.

The HIPC initiative

Selection of the Highly Indebted Poor Countries (HIPCs): 42 countries	Structural adjustment + interim PRSP = > decision point 26 countries had reached it in August 2002	Key reforms imposed by the IMF + final PRSP = > completion point 6 countries had reached it in August 2002

So much for the official side of the story; but we cannot leave it there. It all needs to be closely studied and analysed, in order to understand what is going on in the wings.

The debt was invented by the devil. Go for a walk in Africa and ask where the debt is! No one knows where that debt we are being made to pay comes from. The debt is worse than AIDS. At least with AIDS there is hope for the future, whereas with the debt [...] future generations are condemned to pay it, not even the debt stock, but the interest. I don't talk about the debt because I know we can't get rid of it. They mess about, they reschedule, they throw a few crumbs – it's like giving aspirin to a cancer patient. *Abdoulaye Wade, President of Senegal, in the French daily, Libération, 24 June 2002* (trans. VB)

Q26 What are the results of the HIPC initiative?

By August 2002, twenty-six countries had reached the decision point (*see* Appendix), and six had reached the completion point: Uganda, Bolivia, Mozambique, Tanzania, Burkina Faso and Mauritania.

The IMF, which likes to blow its own trumpet, claimed that the savings made by these twenty-six countries came to $40 billion, without mentioning that they will benefit from this over a period of thirty years in the form of reduced repayments, as we saw for Tanzania. So in order to get a clear picture of the real situation, this sum has to be spread over several decades. According to IMF figures, the annual debt service from now until 2005 will be about 30 per cent lower than it was in 1998. However, as the decision point for these countries was reached in 2000 at the earliest, the effect of the initiative should not be calculated on the years preceding 2001. In reality, the result is different.

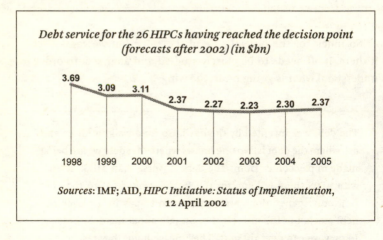

Debt service for the 26 HIPCs having reached the decision point (forecasts after 2002) (in $bn)

1998	1999	2000	2001	2002	2003	2004	2005
3.69	3.09	3.11	2.37	2.27	2.23	2.30	2.37

Sources: IMF; AID, *HIPC Initiative: Status of Implementation*, 12 April 2002

One can see that the debt service drops for the period 1998 to 2001, but for reasons unrelated to the HIPC initiative. The main cause is the traditional mechanism of debt-rescheduling for countries in difficulty (due-dates and certain payments were postponed). The problems are thus deferred until a later date, pushed forward several decades. From 2001, the annual service falls very slightly then

> The hopes being placed on the implementation of the reinforced initiative for the heavily indebted poor countries (HIPCs) are unrealistic. The debt reduction as planned will not be enough to make the debt burden sustainable in the middle term [...]; furthermore, the size of debt reduction and the way it is to be brought into effect will not have any direct result in reducing poverty. *UNCTAD, 2000*

from 2005 it gets back to the 2001 level and starts to climb again. It has been slightly reduced, but by no means will it solve the problem of over-indebtedness for the HIPC.

Officially, the cost of the initiative should be borne by the multilateral institutions for 48 per cent (of which 22 per cent by the World Bank and 7 per cent by the IMF), 48 per cent by the rich countries (of which 38 per cent by the Paris Club members) and 4 per cent by the private banks (which are not much concerned by the debts of the poorest countries, as we saw earlier).

As for the HIPC Trust Fund, the rich states have pledged a total of $2.6 billion. So far, contributions paid in since 1996 come to $1.6 billion (a pittance!). The IMF has contributed by selling off part of its gold reserves ($800 million). As explained above, this money will serve to finance the repayment remissions granted by the multilateral institutions. As a general rule, the IMF and the World Bank are very discreet about how much is in the fund and whether it is enough to finance all the promised reductions. However, they do let it be understood that if the governments do not keep their promises, they will not be able to either.

> It is now widely recognized that, in a certain number of cases, the initial analyses of intolerable indebtedness greatly overestimated the potential of the HIPC in terms of export revenues and economic growth. *Kofi Annan, UN Secretary General's Report on the External Debt Crisis, 2 August 2001*

Q27 What are the limitations of the HIPC initiative?

First, the aim is not to free up development for the HIPCs, but merely to render their debts sustainable. The difference is huge. The idea is to cancel just enough to keep the DCs paying to the maximum of their capabilities. Essentially, it is what could not be paid that is cancelled. The HIPC initiative aims above all to ensure that repayments continue and to dissimulate reinforced structural adjustment beneath a semblance of generosity. In 2000, i.e. four years after the start of the initiative, the forty-two HIPCs transferred colossal sums to the North. The net transfer on the debt was negative for them to the tune of about $2.3 billion.

Second, apart from the fact that it concerns only very small amounts, the HIPC initiative concerns only very few countries. Indeed, to benefit from such reductions, a country must be very poor and very heavily indebted. For example, Nigeria, although very heavily indebted, is nevertheless an oil-producing country, so is not considered poor enough to qualify. As for Haiti, one of the poorest countries on the planet, it is not considered heavily enough indebted to qualify. And the countries where most of the planet's poor live are not concerned: China, India, Indonesia, Brazil, Argentina, Mexico, the Philippines, Pakistan, and so on. How can such an initiative ever hope to get the DCs out of the financial impasse in which they are stuck?

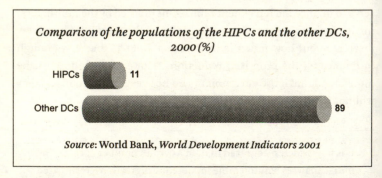

Comparison of the populations of the HIPCs and the other DCs, 2000 (%)

HIPCs — 11

Other DCs — 89

Source: World Bank, *World Development Indicators 2001*

The IMF and the IDA regularly publish reports on the progress of the initiative with projections for the coming years. In the April 2002 report, surprisingly, the HIPC initiative no longer occupied even the small space originally assigned to it. Among the thirty-four countries concerned, several will be overjoyed to learn that their debt service, after a slight and short-lived drop, will then rise again as though nothing had happened. Others will even discover that the reduction so generously granted them will enable them ... to pay more in the years ahead!

Debt service ($m)

	2000	2001	2002 (forecast)	2004 (forecast)
Benin	55	33	34	36
Cameroon	437	271	267	284
Honduras	233	181	209	246
Mali	68	76	86	95
Niger	18	20	37	30
Uganda	90	71	80	102
Zambia	148	149	158	211

Sources: IMF; IDA, *HIPC Initiative: Status of Implementation*, 12 April 2002

Even if, theoretically, any reduction is welcome, living in the economic stranglehold of the IMF is a high price to pay. For the PRSP, which has to be approved by the IMF, does not bear close scrutiny. It is the direct descendant of the infamous structural adjustment programmes of the last twenty years. It has changed in name alone. 'Poverty Reduction Strategy' may sound good, it has a social ring to it, but it is, after all, structural adjustment. A new, but not even improved, SAP. The only difference is a few projects targeting poverty, often incompatible with the imposed growth objectives. No wonder Laos refused to take part.

Officially, the PRSP should be drawn up in concertation with civil society. In practice, this point is often fudged. Certain Non-Governmental Organizations (NGOs) in the South are registered, sometimes without being told, in the different workshops supposed to take part in drawing up the document. They are often given extremely short notice of meetings, or receive the documents at the very last minute. They rarely have time to prepare the meetings with government representatives or the different bodies efficiently. In any case, the latter are in the majority for any decision-making. NGOs outside the capital are not usually consulted. We have even witnessed a minister asking NGOs to sign the document, that is the PRSP, and not to show any disagreement in front of foreigners, so as not to damage the country's credibility. In Burkina Faso, the participation of civil society was limited to a ninety-minute meeting with the 'donors'. Some governments go as far as creating their own NGO to facilitate convergence with civil society. A democratic process of participation? Eyewash.

Adopted by African Heads of State at their Lusaka Summit, without any concertation with social or political representatives, NEPAD has done nothing more than serve up with a new sauce the neo-liberal policies which the Bretton Woods institutions have been imposing for the last three decades, and which have impoverished the populations of the continent [...] Countries applying for the HIPC initiative must adopt a Poverty Reduction Strategy Paper (PRSP), under the auspices of the IMF and the World Bank. This document must indicate the use that will be made of the resources made available by this initiative, and contain a certain number of commitments relating to the implementation of classic structural adjustment measures: privatization of public companies, reduction of the salaried workforce, reduction of grants, elimination of government subsidies, deregulation of the labour market. In other words, the whole arsenal of ultra-liberal measures which have contributed to the impoverishment of African populations, to the degradation of social services, to a fall in life-expectancy of over seven years, to the return of diseases we had thought eradicated, to increased unemployment for young graduates, to setting back industrialization, and to the creation of chronic food shortages. *Moussa Tchangari, 'Un projet néo-libéral pour l'Afrique' [A neo-liberal project for Africa], Alternative (Niger), 24 July 2002* (trans. VB)

The criteria selected to measure the sustainability of the debt pose their own inherent problems.

- They are questionable. How can the decision about whether a country should qualify or not for debt-reduction to fight poverty depend on just a ratio? 149 per cent? Oh! Bad luck! You will just have to manage without, but we do sympathize.
- They are complicated – no doubt on purpose, so that only experts can discuss them, and also the better to conceal the stinginess of the initiative. This time it is their bad luck that there are associations such as the CADTM with international networks whose activists do not hesitate to sniff out the truth and denounce it vehemently. UNCTAD and the UN Human Rights Commission have also published highly critical reports on the initiative.

After nearly two decades of structural adjustment programmes, poverty has increased, growth is mostly slow and erratic, rural crises have deepened and de-industrialization has upset forecasts of growth. For the last two years poverty reduction has become the fundamental aim of the programmes and activities of the international financial institutions in Africa and other countries with low revenue. The change of attitude deserves to be hailed, but has there really been a change of heart? *UNCTAD, press release, 26 September 2002*

The IMF and the World Bank have changed the words, changed the acronyms, changed their methods of consultation, but they have not changed an iota of their creed. *Detlef Kotte, UNCTAD, 'FMI et Banque mondiale: le fiasco africain' [IMF and World Bank: the African fiasco], Libération, 27 September 2002 (trans. VB)*

A detailed examination of the macroeconomic and structural adjustment measures figuring in the PRSPs reveals that the advice formulated in what is known as the 'Washington Consensus' has not been fundamentally questioned. *UNCTAD, 'From Adjustment to Poverty Reduction: What's New?', 26 September 2002*

The flabbergasting 90 per cent cancellation mentioned above and relayed by the media is therefore misleading. As we have seen, it does not affect the whole debt, but it was a clever trick. Far too many people have been taken in. This explains why, if we believe the French government and certain newspapers, France has already cancelled 100 per cent of the debt at least three times. Then countries must show themselves to be politically and economically docile, to be selected. It was perhaps no coincidence that the first country to qualify was Uganda, ally of the United States and the UK in the Great Lakes region of Africa.

> Bilateral agreements have been or must be made with countries with commercial and/or official debts (State loans) towards Belgium. This concerns the following countries: Pakistan, Ghana, Bolivia, Guinea, Madagascar, Cameroon. Only the cancellation of the Bolivian debt has a direct impact on the budget of the Finance Department. This is a sum of 6 million euros, which corresponds to the sum committed in 2001. [...] The other agreements do not entail direct outlay since they take the form of rescheduling over periods of 23 years for the commercial debts and 40 years for the State loans. *The Belgian Treasury's answer to a question put by Claudine Drion on the amounts committed by Belgium in 2001 for debt reduction, June 2002* (trans. VB)

Moreover, it is by no means certain that the sums required for the HIPC Trust Fund to function can be found. Certain multilateral bodies have not yet announced whether or not they will participate in the cancellation and governments are hanging back in keeping their promises. So it is not even certain that the reductions planned for the coming years will be effective. For the time being, the situation is at a standstill.

On the bilateral level, the question of how the sums freed up are counted is crucial. It would be most annoying if that money were deducted from other aid packages given to the DCs. At the moment, there is every reason to be concerned. The case of France is illuminating. France set up a procedure for 'refinancing by donation'. This means that the HIPC repays its instalments to France which quickly transfers the same amount to a special budget line at the Central Bank of the country concerned. How this money will be used is decided by that country's government and the French Ambassador, which means that part of the HIPC's budget is under French trusteeship. Worse still, the amount transferred by France is counted as Official Development Aid, without the ODA having been correspondingly increased. So this non-cancellation (for the bond is not severed between creditor and debtor) takes place to the detriment of projects which were to have been financed by ODA. If this is not a racket, it certainly looks like one.

In fact, the HIPC initiative's main purpose is to strengthen and legitimate the structural adjustment policies imposed by the World Bank and the IMF. The message is, more or less, 'If you adopt the

---

The IMF and the World Bank recognize that the great international programme for debt reduction for the poorest countries will not liberate most of them, as its forecasts have turned out to be over-optimistic. [...] World Bank officials have declared that the Executive Board, which met at the beginning of the week, nevertheless seemed unwilling to show generosity, despite pressure from non-government organizations. [...] The fall in the prices of raw materials has deprived several of the most heavily indebted countries, dependent on the export of agricultural produce, of the hope of reaching their debt–export ratio objectives. The report studies various proposals from NGOs as well as a white paper under examination by the US Congress which aims to increase debt reductions, but it concludes that these initiatives are all too costly and would not generate enough extra funds for the poor countries. [...] Certain rich countries, including Scandinavia and the United Kingdom, have proposed amendments to the programme, with a view to slightly increasing the proposed amount of reduction, but the World Bank officials said that the USA and Japan opposed these modifications, however minor. *'Debt Reduction Programme a Failure, according to IMF', Financial Times (London), 5 September 2002*

policies that we tell you, you will no longer have an unsustainable debt burden. Better still, we will lend you money so that you can carry out the policies we recommend.' It is a new and extremely cunning instrument of domination, which enables the Bretton Woods institutions to shake off all responsibility for increasing indebtedness and get the governments of the South on their side.

No wonder many citizens, especially in the South, think that the HIPC initiative is part of the problem and not part of the solution.

Q28 What is the New Partnership for African Development (NEPAD)?

The decolonization of African countries gave rise to great hope. At last the continent would be able to develop. However, the conditions for such development have not been met, and the social and economic situation has not improved; far from it. The titles of books by the well-known French anti-colonialist and ecologist René Dumont are telling: from *L'Afrique noire est mal partie* [Black Africa makes a bad start] in the 1960s to *L'Afrique étranglée* [Strangled Africa] in 1980, the continent has sunk ever deeper into poverty.

In 1980, the Lagos Plan was drawn up on the initiative of African leaders within the Organization for African Unity (OAU). It aimed to promote endogenous development and industrialization in Africa. Unfortunately it has remained a dead letter, undermined by the Bretton Woods institutions when they launched their structural adjustment programmes, whose objectives were in contradiction with those of the Lagos Plan (*see* Q15 and Q16).

At the end of the 1990s, two authentically African development plans saw the light of day. On the one hand, the Millennium African Plan was initiated by Presidents Thabo Mbeki of South Africa, Olusegun Obasanjo of Nigeria and Abdelaziz Bouteflika of Algeria, on the theme of African renaissance. Since it was a project for independence with regard to the North while respecting African cultural values, it also interested Pan-Africanist circles. On the other hand, the Senegalese President, Abdoulaye Wade, launched the Omega Plan, based on the creation of a blatantly liberal African common market.

These two plans were merged in 2001 to become the New Partnership for African Development (NEPAD). It aims to provide the dynamics needed to fill the gulf that separates Africa from the industrialized countries; in other words, to bring modern practices and economic growth to Africa. Its stock-in-trade is to promote private investment to integrate the continent into world markets. Thus Africa, which represents only 1.7 per cent of world trade (against 5 per cent in 1980), is seen as an open playing field for private initiative. At the Dakar summit in April 2002 on the financing of NEPAD, multinationals of the North, such as Microsoft, Hewlett Packard, Unilever or TotalFinaElf, were very much present.

NEPAD sets out ten priorities, from good governance to access to international markets, from human development to infrastructure. African leaders have also promised to avoid back-sliding and to be vigilant (even though instability and conflict are often partly due to the behaviour of multinationals on the territory [*see* Q44]), thus hoping to enter the good graces of the money-lenders.

NEPAD's founders were received and encouraged by the G8 leaders in 2001 and 2002. This African initiative to attract capital and multinationals, which has won the approval of all the actors of the North, has the effect of legitimating the IMF and World Bank policies across the continent. It is no coincidence that the French representative for dealing with NEPAD is Michel Camdessus, former Director General of the IMF.

The external conditionalities imposed by the IMF through the structural adjustment programmes and described in detail by the press, encounter great reluctance among local populations. The idea is therefore to transform them into internal conditionalities, proposed by the African heads of state themselves. This partnership is a façade which barely conceals the economic submissiveness of Africa, once again.

Sure enough, the projects under consideration within this new framework still bow to the same logic (*see* Q7): a gas pipeline from West Africa or between Algeria and Nigeria; a so-called Transahelian motorway from Dakar to N'Djamena; railway links between Benin, Niger, Burkina Faso and Togo (the Geftarail project); the rehabilitation of the oil refinery in Mombasa (Kenya) and the pipeline at Eldoret; the Grand Inga project to export energy all over the continent, and so on.

Behind this African initiative lies an attempt by four African heads of state in search of recognition to find a place for themselves in the ongoing economic scheme of things. Far from demanding the cancellation of the debts of African states or claiming reparation for centuries of pillage and slavery, NEPAD's main actors, especially Abdoulaye Wade, are a little over-eager to sweep aside such aspirations, preferring to discuss future investments in Africa.

> We have not come here to be offered money. The idea never crossed my mind. The important thing is the commitment made by the G8, which has accepted the new partnership we are proposing. You know, they did not have to receive us. *Abdoulaye Wade, President of Senegal, G8 summit, June 2002*

But while NEPAD's calculations were based on $64 billion of investment a year and a projected growth rate of 7 per cent from now until 2015, these figures are for the time being far from feasible. As was pointed out at the People's Forum in Siby (Mali) in June 2002, foreign private capital prefers to go where the growth is.

> Private capital does not bring growth, but follows it. A cycle of economic development has first to be instigated, if such private capital is to be lured to Africa. Otherwise we are confusing the cherry on the cake with the dough used to bake it! Worse still, if the total amount of capital inflow and outflow is calculated and the results of the WTO rules are factored in, it is Sub-Saharan Africa which is financing the rest of the world, and not the reverse! *Arnaud Zacharie, 'Cerise et commerce mondial' [Cherry and world trade], in Le Soir (Belgium), 4 July 2002* (trans. VB)

On the pretext that it was the moment for action not words, the populations were not consulted. Africans' social, economic and cultural rights, especially those of women, have not been taken into account. African civil society, which cannot possibly be left out, has not been considered either as a force for proposals (in defining alternatives) or as an opposition force to be reckoned with in countering the tendencies towards authoritarianism or neglect of the democratic process. NEPAD certainly seems to have got off on the wrong footing, if it is to bring solutions to the populations of Africa.

> The NEPAD strategy is not to raise issues of repatriation of the money embezzled by African potentates and deposited in foreign accounts, nor of cancellation of the external debt whose service swallows up the best part of the budget of certain countries. [...] In view of the difficult situation the African countries are in, undoubtedly the alternative is to demand the cancellation of the entire external debt, once and for all, and to make use of internal resources, especially by mobilizing savings. The NEPAD document does not give much importance to this issue and proposes no new actions which might end African dependence on external powers [...]
>
> It is scandalous that the African leaders broach neither the crucial question of the reform of the international financial institutions, which impose policies with no regard for the social and economic rights of their countries, nor the question of the modification of unfair world trade rules, with their negative repercussions on people's food security and health. [...] NEPAD should have taken inspiration from the experience of the African delegates' struggle at the failed Seattle talks, and advocated joining forces with the other Third World countries to reverse the negative tendencies of corporate-driven globalization. *Moussa Tchangari, 'Un projet néo-libéral pour l'Afrique' [A neo-liberal project for Africa], in Alternative (Niger), 24 July 2002* (trans. VB)

Q29 What are vulture-funds?

Those DCs which have access to the financial markets issue debt bonds to raise funds. Once issued, the value of these bonds fluctuates according to the economic and financial situation of the country concerned, and can be traded between financial actors.

In recent years, private institutions have sometimes bought up debt bonds issued by countries in difficulty at a low price, sold off by bond-holders who want to try and get some of their initial outlay back. Then this new 'creditor' sues the indebted state in a court of law to demand full and immediate restitution of the loan. Thus they make a colossal profit without a thought for the human and social consequences. These are the infamous 'vulture-funds' which do very well in a context of instability and corruption. The cost to countries is sometimes greater than the small debt reductions they struggle to obtain.

Let us see how Peru was condemned to repay $58 million for bonds bought for $11 million.

The US vulture-fund Elliott Associates paid $11.4 million in 1996 to acquire external Peruvian debt bonds (issued by the Treasury of Peru) with a nominal value of $20.7 million. Elliott Associates bought these bonds on the secondary market, a sort of second-hand market which deals in debt bonds.

Some time later, under the auspices of the Paris Club and the London Club, with the participation of the IMF and the US government, a plan for reducing and restructuring the Peruvian debt was adopted. Elliott Associates refused to take part. They did not want to agree to debt reduction. On the contrary, they demanded that Lima repay the bonds they held at the top rate, plus the unpaid interest, which came to a total of $35 million. Peru refused. Elliott Associates took the litigation before a New York court of law, which in the first instance found them in the wrong. But in 2000 the Court of Appeal gave them satisfaction, even going as far as to accord them priority status, meaning that they should be repaid first. This is extraordinary! Peru was condemned to repay a total of $58 million, as the unpaid interest had continued to accumulate over the four years of the trial. Elliott Associates made a juicy profit of $38 million, their lawyers sharing a modest $9 million between them.

It seems that Elliott Associates were no novices, as they had already played the same game with Panama, Ecuador and Paraguay, getting themselves $130 million along the way.

The moral of the story: a country that 'benefits' from an agreement with its creditors to reduce its debt may then see the latter increase because its financial situation has improved. As its solvency grows, the trade value of the remaining stock goes up. On the other hand, if a country falls behind with repayments, the trade value drops.

The moral of the moral: in a market economy, there are no moral principles. It is wiser to repudiate or cancel the whole debt.

SEVEN

Debt cancellation and suspensions of payment in the past

Q30 Have there ever been debt cancellations in the past?

There have indeed already been debt cancellations in history, some unilateral, some as the result of a legal decision, some conceded by the dominant powers. We present here a few significant cases, which show that it would be possible and beneficial to cancel the present debt, contrary to what the great money-spinners claim.

Debt repudiation
The United States In 1776, the thirteen British colonies of North America decided to constitute the United States and to break away from dependence on the British Crown. The new revolutionary state freed itself from the burden of debt by declaring null and void all debts due to London.

In the nineteenth century, after the election of Abraham Lincoln to the presidency (1860–65), the southern states seceded and constituted the Confederation of American States. The War of Secession that followed (1861–65) saw the victory of the northern states, which were against slavery and in the process of industrialization. At this point, a further debt repudiation took place, this time to the detriment of the wealthy of the southern states. Loans had been contracted in the 1830s, mainly for the creation of banks (Planter's Bank in Mississippi and the Union Bank in North Carolina, in particular) or to underwrite the construction of the railways. In Mississippi, for example, the initial repayments were made but then, in 1852, a law allowed for a referendum that gave the inhabitants the chance to vote for or against the repayment of Planter's Bank bonds. They voted against. After the War of Secession, in 1876, the Constitution was amended by a clause specifically forbidding the repayment of Planter's Bank bonds. The new regime thus legalized the decision to stop repayments. The total amount of repudiated debt in the eight states concerned came to $75 million.

The USSR In January 1918, the brand-new communist USSR refused to take over responsibility for the loans made by Tsarist Russia and cancelled all such debts unconditionally. The new state, born of a revolution that wanted an end to war and to give the land to the peasants, refused to honour loans that had been contracted mainly to pay for the carnage of the First World War. Furthermore, the government wanted to make a clean break from the previous regime.

Mexico and other Latin American countries Already in 1867, Benito Juarez[1] refused to take over the loans that the preceding regime of the Emperor Maximilian had contracted with the French bank, the Société Générale de Paris, two years earlier to finance the occupation of Mexico by the French Army.

In 1914, in the middle of the revolution, when Emiliano Zapata[2] and Pancho Villa[3] were on the offensive, Mexico suspended its external debt payments completely. Thus the most heavily indebted country on the continent reimbursed only symbolic amounts, to keep the peace, between 1914 and 1942. Between 1922 and 1942 (twenty years!), negotiations took place with a consortium of creditors led by one of the managers of the J. P. Morgan Bank of the United States. Between 1934 and 1940, President Lázaro Cárdenas[4] nationalized without compensation the petroleum industry and the

---

1 Benito Juárez Garciá (1806–72) was a Mexican statesman of Amerindian origin. In 1861, elected to the presidency, he set up la Reforma, which was liberal and anti-clerical. From 1863, he fought French intervention in Mexico and had the Emperor Maximilian shot in 1867.

2 Emiliano Zapata (1879–1919) was a Mexican revolutionary. A peasant leader, he led radical struggles and, in 1911, helped to draw up a vast programme of social change, known as the Ayala Project. In 1914, as an ally of Pancho Villa, he dominated the Mexican revolutionary scene and occupied the Mexican capital. He was assassinated in 1919.

3 Pancho Villa (1878–1920) was a Mexican revolutionary who led the Division del Norte (Northern Army). He was assassinated in 1920.

4 Lázaro Cárdenas (1895–1970), a general, was elected to the presidency in December 1934.

railways, which were in the hands of British and North American companies. He also expropriated more than 18 million hectares of the great landed estates known as *latifundia*, belonging to national and foreign owners, and distributed them in the form of 'communal property' (*ejido*). He also completely overhauled the public education system.

Naturally, the creditors (mostly from the United Kingdom and the United States) howled in protest at these radical, anti-imperialist, popular policies. But Mexico's tenacity paid off. In 1942, the creditors renounced about 80 per cent of the value of the debts (in their 1914 state, i.e. they also renounced the back interest) and made do with small compensation deals for the companies that had been expropriated. Other countries, such as Brazil, Bolivia and Ecuador, also suspended part or all of their repayments from 1931. In the case of Brazil, the selective suspension of repayments went on until 1943, when an agreement brought the debt down by 30 per cent. Ecuador, too, stopped paying from 1931 until the 1950s.

In the 1930s, a total of fourteen countries suspended payments over a prolonged period. Of all the heavily indebted, only Argentina kept up with its payments without interruption. It was also the Latin American country with the poorest economic results in the 1930s.

Suspensions through favourable arbitration

Cuba In 1898, the United States had won a war against Spain to gain control of Cuba (until then a Spanish colony). Cuba was separated from the Spanish Crown, as were Puerto Rico and the Philippines, which also became US protectorates. After the war, Cuba was asked by Spain to repay its debt. The same year, a conference was held in Paris to deal with the problem, and the USA contended that the debt was odious, since it had been imposed by Spain in its own interests, without the consent of the Cuban people. Spain accepted the argument and Cuba did not have to pay this colonial debt.

Turkey Between 1889 and 1902, Turkey went through a deep financial crisis which rendered it incapable of honouring its debts towards Tsarist Russia. In 1912 the International Court of Arbitration recognized the government of Turkey's plea of '*force majeure*' as well founded.

Costa Rica In September 1919, the Tinoco government in Costa Rica, considered illegitimate by the United States but recognized by other states including Great Britain, was overthrown. In August 1922, the new government renounced all contracts signed by its predecessor, and especially with its main creditor, the Royal Bank of Canada. Judge Taft, President of the Supreme Court of the United States, who had to arbitrate in 1923, found in favour of annulment. So the new government of Costa Rica did not have to repay the debt.

> The transaction in question was concluded at a time when the Tinoco government had lost the confidence of the people and when the political and military movement preparing to overthrow the government was gaining strength. The Royal Bank affair does not hinge on the form of transaction, but rather concerns the Bank's good faith. It behoved the Bank to prove that it provided the government with money for a truly legitimate purpose. This it has failed to do. We cannot consider that the Royal Bank of Canada has proved that the money paid was indeed destined for legitimate use by the government. Consequently, its claim must be rejected. *Judge Taft, 1923, quoted in P. Adams, Odious Debts, 1991*

Cancellation conceded by the dominant powers
Poland In 1919, the Treaty of Versailles at the end of the First World War considered that the debt contracted by Germany to colonize Poland could not be imputed to the newly constituted Polish state. Poland did not, therefore, have to repay it.

Germany In 1953, the London agreement decided on the cancellation of 51 per cent of Germany's war debt. The idea was that the debt service should not exceed 3.5 per cent of its export revenues, a percentage that is far exceeded nowadays by the DCs which pay an average of over 17 per cent! Yet Germany did not fulfil any of the criteria required at present to qualify for a reduction; and its dictatorship of the preceding decade had sown death and destruction in a large part of the world. The cancellation was very beneficial for Germany, which later became the leading economy in Europe and the locomotive of European construction.

Namibia and Mozambique Highly aware of the consequences of the long Apartheid regime which had damaged the whole region, South Africa unilaterally and unconditionally cancelled its debt claims on Namibia in 1995 and Mozambique in 1999.

Procedures undertaken by the DCs over the last twenty years

The year 1985 was an eventful one in Latin America.

In July 1985, the new President of Peru, Alan Garcia, decided to limit debt repayments to 10 per cent of export revenues. This led to Peru's banishment from the international community by the IMF and the World Bank, under the impetus of the USA, causing isolation and destabilization. The experiment lasted only a few months and the arrears on the interest, estimated at some $5 billion, were directly added to the debt stock (capitalization of interest).

Again in July 1985, at a conference in Havana (Cuba), Fidel Castro launched an appeal for non-payment of the debt and for the constitution of a Latin American and Caribbean Continental Front. The front was under discussion but the governments of Mexico, Brazil and Colombia managed to scuttle it, due to pressure exerted by the USA behind the scenes.

In 1986, at a meeting of the Organization for African Unity (OAU), Thomas Sankara, the young President of Burkina Faso, also pronounced himself in favour of unilateral cancellation of the debt and the constitution of an African Front of refusal to pay.

On 15 November 1987, Thomas Sankara was assassinated. Since then not a single African head of state has taken up the torch of repudiation of the debt.

Ten years later, in 1997, South Korea, hit by the crisis, was very firm: it would continue payments, provided that the foreign creditors continued with their loans. Thus it imposed the debt restructuring it wanted, without being banished.

The rare cases of firmness have had very positive results for the indebted countries. So what if democratically elected governments

> The debt cannot be repaid, firstly because if we do not pay, the money-lenders will certainly not die of it; on the other hand, if we pay, we shall, with equal certainty, die. [...] Those who have led us into debt have gambled as though in a casino. When they were winning, there was no debate. Now that they have lost through gambling, they demand that we repay them. And there is talk of a crisis. They have gambled, they have lost, those are the rules of the game. Life goes on. [...] If Burkina Faso is alone in refusing to repay the debt, I will not be present at the next conference. *Thomas Sankara, 1986, speech addressed to the OAU at Addis-Ababa (Ethiopia)* (trans. VB)

supported by citizens' movements decreed a freeze on repayments? There is an urgent need for citizens to get to grips with the debt problem everywhere they can, and to push their governments to take such steps.

Several 'People's Tribunals' against the debt have been held in recent years. In December 2000, the international conference 'Africa: from Resistance to Alternatives' was held in Dakar, associating social movements from North and South, including the Senegalese association CONGAD (Conseil des ONG d'appui au développement, or the Council of NGOs in Support of Development) and the CADTM. A group of women from the suburbs of Dakar wrote and performed *Le Procès de la dette* [The Debt on Trial] with the IMF, the World Bank, the G7 and the governments of the South standing accused. Women who were victims in their daily life of the structural adjustment programmes were questioned as witnesses. The involvement of the entire population – young people, women, athletes, trade unionists and so on – was remarkable throughout the conference, and gave this particular event an impressive resonance. In February 2002, at the World Social Forum at Porto Alegre, the International People's Tribunal on the Debt was held, at the initiative of the international network, Jubilee South (*see* Q38), in collaboration with the CADTM. These two examples show the need felt by the populations of the South, who endure the hardships caused by the debt, to see judged and condemned (symbolically for the moment) those responsible for the iniquitous system.

Furthermore, several attempts to allow the population to express their opinion democratically on the debt mechanism have been made. In Spain, during the general elections in March 2000, a 'Social Consultation' was held, calling for a vote on the abolition of the external debts owed by the DCs to the Spanish state. Despite the enormous difficulties made by the public authorities, which declared the consultation illegal, the referendum enabled over a million people to vote, of whom over 95 per cent were in favour of abolition. Then in Brazil, in September 2000, during the National Week which ends with National Independence Day and the '*Grito de los excluidos*' [Shouts of the Forsaken] with the march of the landless and the unemployed, 6 million people also took part, all over the country, in a similar kind of consultation, and 95 per cent voted to stop the repayment of the Brazilian debt. These initiatives are valuable in popularizing the struggle against debt and allowing the populations to express their anger.

Q31 Why do the governments of the South continue to repay the debt?

Since the debt crisis of the early 1980s, the DCs have become dependent on loans from the international financial institutions. So the latter have an efficient means of putting on pressure. This is why Southern governments that still have the will to oppose the Washington Consensus are few and far between. Even East Timor, which has only had true independence since May 2002, was immediately incited to run up debts, against the wishes of its leaders.

This pressure, as we have seen, is facilitated by a system of case-by-case negotiations which keeps the indebted state in a constant position of weakness, unlike the perfectly organized creditors: the IMF, the World Bank, the Paris Club, the London Club and so on.

The DCs' governments prefer to get their loans from the international institutions rather than risk being banished from the international community.

Moreover, the rich countries know very well how to use all their influence and skill to get the men they trust into power, at the head of DCs. These dignitaries of the South have often received considerable financial and logistical support and, once in power, knowing to whom they owe it, they promote the interests of their precious protectors. The CIA is rarely foreign to any accession to power in Latin America (as in Colombia or Nicaragua in 2001–02); the France–Africa connection is omnipresent in French-speaking Africa, whenever the question of imposing or maintaining a president arises (like Idriss Déby in Chad in May 2001 or Denis Sassou Nguesso in Congo-Brazzaville in March 2002). President Hugo Chavez of Venezuela is seen as a lucky survivor since the failed *coup d'état* in April 2002 which nearly succeeded in carrying the country's top businessman to power, quickly recognized by Spain and the United States. They had not reckoned with the pressure of the street demonstrations which returned Chavez.

> The issue of the moral responsibility of the creditors was particularly apparent in the case of Cold War loans. When the IMF and the World Bank lent money to the Democratic Republic of Congo's notorious leader, Mobutu, they knew (or should have known) that most of that money would not go to help that country's poor people, but rather would be used to enrich Mobutu. It was money paid to ensure that this corrupt leader would keep his country aligned with the West. To many, it doesn't seem fair for ordinary tax-payers of countries with corrupt governments to have to repay loans that were made to leaders that did not represent them.
> *Joseph Stiglitz, Globalization and Its Discontents, 2002*

To complete the picture, most finance officials in the countries of the South are graduates of the top business schools or universities of the North (Harvard, Columbia, Princeton, Oxford, Cambridge) and have been baked in the liberal mould. The Governor of the Central Bank of Brazil, Arminio Fraga Neto, formerly managed an investment fund for the financier Georges Soros. The Ivorian Alassane Dramane Ouattara was Director of the Africa Department of the IMF from 1984 to 1988 before becoming Prime Minister of the Republic of Ivory Coast from 1990 to 1993, then assistant Director General of the IMF from 1994 to 1999. At the time of the crisis in Turkey in February 2001, the most symbolic gesture of the international financial institutions was to lend (along with money) Kemal Dervis, then Vice-President of the World Bank, who became the Minister of Finance in his country. Vicente Fox, the Mexican President elected in 2000, had previously been the manager of the Mexican subsidiary of Coca-Cola. Alejandro Toledo was a consultant employed by the World Bank before becoming President of Peru in 2001. Is it any wonder that the policies followed conform perfectly to the wishes of Washington?

The populations in the South are never seriously consulted and are kept carefully out of the picture. The system functions in isolation, and has ways and means of bringing most of the recalcitrant countries to see 'reason'. The others will be martyrs.

EIGHT

The case for cancelling the DCs' debts

Q32 Will debt cancellation be enough to ensure the development of the DCs?

First of all, let us state that the repayment of a loan contracted in regular and reasonable conditions is a moral obligation. However, the present debt crisis, which is striking down the DCs, must be considered in quite another context. The moral obligation to repay, which usually exists, collapsed when the trap closed over the DCs in the early 1980s and annihilated all hope of development. It is absolutely not a case of wriggling out of a legitimate obligation, becoming an outlaw beyond the pale of morality. It is a question of taking account of the mechanisms of domination, pillage and wretched poverty that the DCs endure to demand a measure of justice.

> The peoples of the Third World must repay a debt which they never profited from and whose benefits never reached them. *Adolfo Perez Esquivel, Nobel Peace Prize-winner, 1980*

The system set up by the industrialized states using the IMF and the World Bank has ensured their domination over the DCs. The debt is its nerve centre. We are going to review the many arguments in favour of total cancellation of the external public debt of the

> Recently, attention has focused on debt-forgiveness, and for good reason. Without the forgiveness of debt, many of the developing countries simply cannot grow. Huge proportions of their current exports go to repaying loans to the developed countries. *Joseph Stiglitz, Globalization and Its Discontents, 2002*

DCs. Jubilee South is right to proclaim: 'We owe nothing, we will pay nothing.' But putting the counters back to zero will not in itself modify the system which has led to this deadlock. Debt cancellation is a necessary but insufficient condition. From that point on, alternative mechanisms for financing must be established, which do not lead to debt-induced submissiveness, and important complementary measures must be taken in numerous areas (*see* Q43).

Q33 What are the moral arguments in favour of cancelling the DCs' debts?

We have seen that the debt leads the states of the South, often generously provided with human and natural wealth, to a general state of impoverishment due to organized looting and pillage, of which the debt mechanism is the linchpin.

Repaying the debt is an essential obstacle to satisfying basic human needs, such as access to clean water, decent food, basic healthcare, primary education, decent accommodation and satisfactory infrastructure. Without doubt, the satisfaction of basic human needs must take priority over all other considerations, be they geopolitical or financial. From a moral point of view, the rights of creditors, stockholders or speculators are insignificant in comparison with the fundamental rights of 5 billion citizens.

It is immoral to demand of the DCs that they devote their meagre resources to repaying well-heeled creditors (whether in the North or the South) rather than to the satisfaction of these fundamental needs.

The debt is one of the main mechanisms whereby economic colonization operates to the detriment of the DCs. It is one more brick in the wall of historic abuses, also carried out by the rich countries: slavery, the pillage of raw materials and cultural goods, the extermination of indigenous populations, the colonial yoke and so on. The time is overdue to replace the logic of domination by the logic of redistribution of wealth in the name of justice.

The IMF, the World Bank and the Paris Club impose their own truth, their own justice, and they make the rules. It is time to finish with this phoney justice of conquerors and oppressors.

The debt is immoral because it was frequently contracted by

Eight

118

undemocratic regimes, who did not use the money received in the interests of their populations, and who often organized embezzlement on a massive scale with the tacit or active agreement of the states of the North, the World Bank and the IMF. The creditors of the industrialized countries, who took advantage of the high interest rates in 1979 and the low prices of raw materials on the international market, knowingly lent money to often corrupt regimes. They have no right to demand that the people repay such loans. Let them address the fallen dictators, or those still in place, and their accomplices.

Let us risk a comparison. The activists who fought throughout history against slavery were moved by an ideal of justice and were fiercely opposed to the abominable practice. The time came when the citizens' struggle brought about a change in the power balance, and made the abolition of slavery unavoidable, despite the forecasts of economic disaster made by those who defended slavery. In the case of the external public debt of the DCs and the turn of events since 1980, the situation is comparable (though not identical). The debt has become an implacable mechanism of domination whose hidden workings need first to be understood. The protests of citizens revolted by this overweening domination and its human ravages must intensify to break the stranglehold.

The North cannot expect that its (relative) well-being should be financed by poverty in the South. Demanding the total cancellation of the external public debt for all the DCs is simply coming to the

> The countries in the South must stop repaying their debt. That debt is illegitimate, since in most cases it was contracted by totalitarian and corrupt governments who embezzled the money for their own profit. It is also the result of the pillage of our wealth by the North during centuries of exploitation. The populations of the South no longer have to bear such a burden, which remains an instrument of domination and control by the rich countries over the poorest. *Lidy Napcil, international co-ordinator of Jubilee South, 'Jubilé Sud: les tribunaux de la dette' [Jubilee South: the debt on trial], Le Monde, 26 January 2002* (trans. VB)

rescue of peoples in danger. It has to be total, for slavery cannot be amended, it has to be abolished.

Q34 What are the political arguments in favour of cancelling the DCs' debts?

The mechanisms of the debt cycle have subjected the DCs to the demands of Washington (where the IMF, the World Bank and the US Treasury are all found). Most of its economic policy is decided outside the country concerned. Now there is no valid reason why the IMF and the World Bank should interfere in every economic decision a DC makes. The debt enables the creditors to exercise exorbitant power over the indebted countries. It has enabled the dominant classes of the North to overcome the rest of the world. It is a modern form of slavery.

The DCs which have been subjected to the stranglehold of the creditors represented by the IMF and the World Bank have gradually been forced to abandon all sovereignty. Governments no longer have the power to put in place the policies for which they were elected. In Guyana, for example, the government had decided, in early 2000, to increase the salaries of the civil service by 3.5 per cent, after a fall in purchasing power of 30 per cent in the preceding five years. The IMF immediately threatened to remove it from the list of HIPCs. After a few months, the government had to back-pedal.

On the other hand, in the summer of 2002, Brazil, the Third World country with the most voluminous debt, was shaken by particularly bad financial turbulence due to the combined contagious effects of the Argentine crisis and the economic slow-down in the US and the European Union. President Cardoso's government negotiated an agreement with the IMF which granted them a gigantic loan of a size never seen before: $30.4 billion by the end of 2003, to be added to the existing external debt of $238 billion. Naturally there was a snag: the IMF demanded that a strict austerity budget should be adhered to until 2005. This loan, destined to calm down the markets, was also a means of reining in the future government. The IMF exacted an agreement in principle on this plan from the main presidential candidates before granting the loan. Magnanimously, it relented on its initial insistence on a written agreement. The IMF director, the German Horst

Köhler, is clear: 'By reducing vulnerability and incertitude, the new programme [...] provides the new government with a bridge for after 2003.' Conclusion: the IMF directly interferes in the internal politics of a country with a view to influencing the choice of its citizens.

The citizens of the South, from Senegal to Argentina, know the IMF and the World Bank, and experience the destructive effects of the structural adjustment programmes every day of their lives. In Senegal, one often hears in the street remarks like, 'President Wade is getting senile. One day he announces new measures and the next he does the opposite.' No, no, Abdoulaye Wade is not senile. He is simply under the thumb of the IMF and the World Bank who do not hesitate to impose such-and-such a measure upon him or to forbid such-and-such. He has to do as he is told. The decisions are made at a higher level.

True sovereignty will remain an impossible dream for the DCs for as long as they stay under the yoke of the IMF and the World Bank, and more generally of all the creditors of the North.

After five centuries of pillage, slavery and colonization and twenty years of structural adjustment programmes, the populations of the South have a right to demand reparation for all the ills they have suffered, caused by an invisible mechanism set up by the creditors of the North with the support of the ruling classes of the South. Total cancellation of the debt should be the first act of reparation.

Globalization, as it has been advocated, often seems to replace the old dictatorships of national elites with new dictatorships of international finance. Countries are effectively told that if they don't follow certain conditions, the capital markets or the IMF will refuse to lend them money. They are basically forced to give up part of their sovereignty, to let capricious capital markets, including the speculators whose only concerns are short-term rather than the long-term growth of the country and the improvement of living standards, 'discipline' them, telling them what they should and should not do. *Joseph Stiglitz, Globalization and Its Discontents, 2002*

I must say yet again what I have not ceased to repeat since 1985. The debt has already been amply repaid, given the terms under which it was contracted, the arbitrary and vertiginous growth of interest rates on the dollar during the preceding decade and the fall in prices of the basic products which are the fundamental source of revenue for countries still needing to develop. The debt has become a self-perpetuating vicious circle where new debts are taken out to pay off the interest on standing ones. It is clearer than ever that the debt is not an economic problem, but a political one, and it is as such that it must be resolved. The solution has to come mainly from those who have the resources and the power to do it: the rich countries. This can no longer be ignored. *Fidel Castro, Cuban Head of State, in a speech in Havana, 12 April 2000*

Too many inhabitants of the rich countries do not understand these perverse mechanisms which drive inhabitants of the DCs to leave their land and their loved ones to try to survive in the North. They often have no alternative, since the wealth they produce is systematically sucked up by the North. Aid sent by the rich countries is far too meagre even to begin to compensate this transfer of wealth from the South. The grotesque rise of egotism, which can be commonly observed in Europe, with its attendant racism and xenophobia, is a consequence of the ignorance of some and the bad faith of others. There is a pressing need to lift the veil and explain that it is in the common interests of the populations of North and South alike to unite in demanding the total cancellation of the external public debt, on the one hand, and an end to structural adjustment programmes, on the other.

Q35 What are the economic arguments in favour of cancelling the DCs' debts?

On the one hand, the figures given (*see* Q22) prove that the debt has already been repaid several times over. To date, for every $1 owed in 1980, the DCs have repaid $7.5 and still owe $4. The debt is no longer the cause of fair repayment of a loan obtained under regular conditions, but a very clever instrument of domination, dissimulating, racketeering and pillage.

On the other hand, the net transfers concerning the debt are strongly negative for the South. Since 1995, the governments of the different DCs have 'given' a total contribution of about $250 billion to capital-holders in the North, resulting from the work of local salary-earners and producers. This financial haemorrhage due to the debt, which is bleeding the countries of the South and the East dry, has to be stopped.

Instead, a cycle of ecologically sustainable and socially just development must be promoted. The iniquitous debt must be abolished, and mechanisms established for alternative funding of development, and effective restraints on the tendency to borrow.

The economies of the South have everything to gain through the cancellation of their external debt. Examples of actual cancellations carried out in the past have proved particularly beneficial for the economies of the countries concerned (*see* Q30).

The economies of the South would not be forced, as they are today, to export at all costs to repay their debt. This very fact has already caused impressive falls in the prices of raw materials on the world market, forcing them down to unacceptable levels.

The DCs could also give priority to relations between each other, instead of always seeking markets in the North to earn strong currencies. Countries of the South could set up a graduated form of protectionism. Since the San Jose agreements, this has already come about for petroleum products, which Venezuela provides to thirteen Latin American countries at preferential rates (20 per cent reduction). Cartels could be created between countries dealing in certain kinds of produce so that they could influence prices and world trade, rather like OPEC (*see* Glossary) with petroleum. Then the DCs could at last enjoy acceptable prices for their production, and would be better able to preserve their non-renewable resources (mines, petroleum, gas, fish stocks and so on).

Furthermore, infrastructures and essential public services are powerful factors of endogenous growth. Private investment loses its efficacy when there is no appropriate public investment. Growth is an indispensable premise for attracting private capital (*see* Q28). Yet any substantial public investment is made impossible by the weight of the debt and the obligatory budgetary austerity that goes with it. Cancelling the debt, therefore, can play a powerful role in restarting the world economy.

> Following a rise in the price of oil decided by OPEC: 'A top Western official telephoned me from far away to say that he was concerned by the price of oil. I replied, "So am I! But why don't we discuss the debt of the poor countries, too, and the unfairness of the terms of the exchange?"' *Hugo Chavez, President of Venezuela, Libération, September 2000* (trans. VB)

Q36 What are the legal arguments in favour of cancelling the DCs' debts?

There are several arguments in International Law that can be invoked as legal justification for unilateral cancellation of the external debt. Three of them are outlined below.

The case of force majeure

Force majeure can be invoked when a government or public body finds itself, due to external circumstances beyond its control, unable to fulfil its international obligations, including the repayment of a debt. This is the juridical codification of the fact that no one can be expected to do the impossible, something which is clear both in International Law and common sense. The external and unintentional circumstances may very well be a fall in the prices of raw materials or an action on the part of the creditors (who are recognized as being co-responsible in the mechanism of indebtedness by the law), or again the rise in interest rates in 1979. The DCs contracted loans at reasonable rates in the 1970s, but the actions of the rich countries aimed at greatly increasing interest rates and manoeuvring to lower the prices of raw materials on the world market have radically changed the nature of the deal. This is indeed a case of *force majeure* caused by the unilateral behaviour of the industrialized countries.

The state of necessity

This is characterized by a situation where the existence of the state is endangered, that is, its economic or political survival. Such a situation might be grave social upheaval or the impossibility of fulfilling the needs of the population (health, education, and so on). Here, it is not a matter of being absolutely prevented from fulfilling international obligations, but to do so would necessitate sacrifices on the part of the population which go beyond what is reasonable. The *state of necessity* may justify repudiating the debt, as it implies prioritizing the different obligations of the state.

The United Nations Human Rights Commission has adopted numerous resolutions on the issue of the debt and structural adjustment. One such resolution, adopted in 1999, asserts that 'the exercise of the fundamental rights of the population of an indebted country to food, housing, clothing, work, education, healthcare services and a healthy environment, may not be subordinated to the application of structural adjustment policies or economic reforms generated by the debt'.

The DCs are no longer able to fulfil the fundamental human needs of their populations. This inability throws into question the very existence of all these states, which must invoke the 'state of necessity' for the unilateral cessation of their repayments.

> A State cannot be expected to close its schools, its universities, its courts of law, and to abandon its public services to the point of chaos and anarchy in the community, simply to keep the money for repaying its foreign or national creditors. *Directory of the U.N. Commission on International Law, vol. I, 1980*

Odious debts

International Law recognizes the need to take into account the nature of the regime that contracted the debts, and the use the funds thus raised were put to. This implies the direct responsibility of the creditors, such as private bodies or the IFI. If a dictatorial regime is replaced by a legitimate regime, the latter can demonstrate that the debts were not contracted in the interests of the nation or were, but for odious ends. In this case, they can be declared null and void, and the new government does not have to repay them. The creditors should pursue their case with the leaders of the dictatorship, on a personal basis. The IMF, the World Bank or any other creditor is legally obliged to check that the loans made are put to legitimate use, especially when they cannot help but know that they are dealing with an illegitimate regime.

Argentina, after the dictatorship that ended in 1984, was perfectly justified in taking this route. The Olmos judgment of 13 July 2000, pronounced before the Criminal and Correctional Court no. 2, recognized that the policies carried out over seven years could be defined as legally organized pillage, with the active participation of the IMF and the World Bank. But it was no good. Enormous pressure was put on the Argentine government until they finally agreed to take on the debt to the very last peso ... until 2001 when, after more than three years of recession, they were completely unable to pay, following the refusal of the IMF to grant a further loan.

This point could also have been used by many other governments that succeeded illegitimate regimes, such as in Latin America after the fall of the military dictatorships (Uruguay, Brazil, Chile, and so on), the Philippines after the departure of Marcos in 1986, Rwanda after the genocide in 1994, South Africa at the end of Apartheid, Zaire after the overthrow of Mobutu in 1997 or Indonesia at the fall of Suharto in 1998. One can only deplore that the governments that replaced the dictatorships capitulated before the creditors in taking on previous debts, however odious, and found themselves prisoners of repayments they could have avoided. In doing this, they have unduly burdened their people. Their choice has had a negative impact on the daily lives of several successive generations. The leaders chose what was easiest for them. In exchange for their docility and their cowardice, the creditors (whether they be the Bretton Woods institutions or private bankers) have lent them more money. Governments do not repay out of their personal money boxes; it is the population who have to sacrifice their meagre resources. Today all these governments can find to do is negotiate rescheduling or small reductions.

The notion of odious debt has been invoked, though, on occasion, as in Cuba in 1898, Costa Rica in 1922, Namibia in 1995 and Mozambique in 1999 (*see* Q30). When the notion is successfully invoked, the state debt becomes the personal debt of those responsible during the dictatorship, and cannot engage the financial resources of the state. These notions urgently need to be brought to the heart of public debate, to incite the democratic governments of the DCs to take such a course whenever possible.

Thus International Law is rich in doctrines which could provide grounds, and indeed have already provided grounds, for the cancellation or repudiation of debts. The social movements must insist that International Law, and especially the Universal Declaration of Human Rights and the Pact for Social, Cultural and Economic Rights must take precedence over the rights of creditors and usurers. These foundation texts can in no sense be compatible with the repayment of an immoral, and often odious, debt.

If a despotic power contracts a debt, not according to the needs and interests of the State, but to fortify the despotic regime, to put down the population which would combat it, this debt is odious for the population of the entire State. This debt is not binding for the nation, it is the debt of a regime, the personal debt of the power which contracted it. Consequently, it falls when that power falls. *Alexander Nahum Sack, Les effets des transformations des États sur leurs dettes publiques et autres obligations financières [The effects of the transformations of States on their public debts and other financial obligations], Recueil Sirey 1927* (trans. VB)

Q37 What are the environmental arguments in favour of cancelling the DCs' debts?

The two main causes of the degradation of the natural environment are well known. At one pole of the planet, there is accumulation of the wealth produced with no regard for the balance of the ecosystems, to the point that certain resources are near exhaustion. At the other, the poverty is such that it condemns populations to surrender their resources to the highest bidder.

On the one hand, in the rich countries, overproduction and over-consumption rule. Natural resources are exploited well beyond their capacity for renewal. Indeed, overall, we humans consume 40 per cent more resources than we can produce on a sustainable basis.

All this has very harmful side-effects: air and water pollution, the accumulation of highly toxic waste, the disappearance of green areas. When they can, the governments and multinationals of the North who are responsible for the degradation try to get the DCs to bear the brunt of it. For example, US industrial waste containing heavy metals is sent to India to be processed. The vice-like grip of the debt obliges the DCs to accept the highly pollutant industries of the North. The subjugation of the South through the debt mechanism contributes to its becoming the dustbin for the North.

When it comes to exporting pollution, the cynicism of the leaders of the North with regard to the populations of the South sometimes beggars belief.

In the DCs, for several centuries, the resources have been exploited to the exclusive profit of the ruling classes of the rich countries. One only has to think of the tons of precious metals which have been taken from Latin America to Europe since the sixteenth century or the ravages of colonization in Africa and Asia. Force, needed at the time to seize all these riches, has now been replaced by structural adjustment programmes. To obtain the hard currency needed to repay the debt or keep themselves in power, governments are ready to overexploit and sell off their natural resources (minerals, petroleum, fishing), putting biodiversity at risk (many species of animals and plants are becoming extinct), encouraging deforestation, soil-erosion and desertification (*see* Q2 and Q4). In Africa, 65 per cent of arable land has been degraded over the last fifty years, i.e. 500 million hectares of land.

The shortage of sanitation, drinking water or fuel is a great problem. Untreated rubbish is often tipped into the nearest sea or river. At the moment, fourteen African countries are short of water, even in normal conditions, and it is estimated that this number will reach twenty-five by 2025. Dangerous substances, used for example to treat minerals (such as mercury in goldmines) are released without any precautions, poisoning watercourses and ultimately the groundwater.

Faced with looming ecological emergencies, in 1997 world leaders

> The under-populated countries of Africa are largely under-polluted. Their air quality is unnecessarily good compared to Los Angeles or Mexico [...] There needs to be greater migration of pollutant industries towards the least developed countries [...] and greater concern about a factor increasing the risk of prostate cancer in a country where people live long enough to get the disease, than in a country where 200 children per thousand die before the age of five.
>
> The idea that we should impose limits on growth because of natural limits is a grave error; moreover, it is an idea whose social cost would be stupefying, if ever it were applied.
>
> The economic logic according to which we should get rid of toxic waste by sending it to the countries with the lowest salaries seems to me irreproachable.
>
> Environmental problems are serious everywhere, but only in poor countries do they kill and maim millions of people each year, along with the other terrible effects of poverty. Any environmental strategy which slows down the growth of the poor countries, either by direct regulation or by limiting their markets is perfectly immoral.
>
> *Lawrence Summers, Chief Economist at the World Bank, 1991 (later Secretary of State to the Treasury under US President Bill Clinton)*

tried to establish the organized reduction of greenhouse gases, with the Kyoto Agreement. This planned a reduction in emissions of 5.2 per cent so that by 2008–12 we would be back at 1990 levels. Yet there is a struggle to get even such a moderate initiative. Australia and the United States refuse to contemplate the slightest constraint in this area (*see* Q2). There is even a system of gas emission rights under way, whereby countries which do not emit their full 'quota' will be able to sell their rights to those who tend to exceed the agreed levels. The aim is simply to find a way of not imposing restrictions on the industrialized countries.

Instead of setting up a market of polluting rights, on the pretext that poor countries will be able to make money by selling their permits, it would be much better to have done with the spiral of debt mechanisms, cancel the debt and thus give the indebted countries the chance to fulfil their needs by using non-pollutant and non-wasteful methods of production.

Because of the irreversible damage to the environment, mainly in the poor countries, we hold that an environmental debt has been mounting up over several decades, owed by the industrialized states to the populations of the DCs. Substantial reparation must therefore be demanded.

The structural adjustment programmes demanded by the creditors lead to policies which, structurally, end up by degrading the environment because they remove from the state the responsibility for managing the territory, its natural resources and the ecological balance for the common good. The SAPs transfer this responsibility to private groups, often multinationals, which have no immediate interest in the public good. Their objective is to make the maximum profit in the shortest time possible.

Environmental conditions are therefore grossly neglected in the present system, where economic, financial and geopolitical interests are the only ones that count. Cancelling the debt and letting populations decide for themselves at last how to use the funds that concern them is the only way to integrate ecological issues into the notion of development.

Q38 What are the religious arguments in favour of cancelling the DCs' debts?

The various religions of the Book have all addressed the problem of debt, in their prescriptions.

The Bible

The Bible contains the notion of Jubilee, which consists of an exceptional year every fifty years when debts are annulled or 'forgiven'.

This Jubilee year is marked by social measures such as letting the land lie fallow, freeing slaves and remitting debts.

> And let seven Sabbaths of years be numbered to you, seven times seven years; even the days of seven Sabbaths of years, that is forty-nine years. Then let the loud horn be sounded far and wide on the tenth day of the seventh month; on the day of taking away sin let the horn be sounded through all your land. And let this fiftieth year be kept holy, and say publicly that everyone in the land is free from debt: it is the Jubilee, and every man may go back to his heritage and to his family. *Leviticus 25: 8–10*

Thus money-lending is legitimate for reasons of subsistence, on condition that there is no interest charged and that the loan does not exceed seven years. At the end of this period, the debt is remitted. If someone's situation deteriorates so much that he has to sell himself into bondage to survive, and become a slave, he must be freed after seven years.

The Qur'an

According to the founding text of Islam, the domain of trade and exchange must be marked by a moral, social and therefore a religious dimension. Usury – the practice of lending for interest – called '*riba*', is thus rejected. Islam considers it to be an unfair practice, since the difficulties of the borrower can enable the lender to get rich without any effort.

> Allah has allowed trading and forbidden usury. *II, v. 275*
>
> And if (the debtor) is in straitness, then let there be postponement until he is in ease; and that you remit it as alms is better for you, if you knew. *II, v. 280*
>
> O you who believe! Do not devour usury, making it double and redouble, and be careful of [your duty to] Allah, that you may be successful! *III, v. 130*

This is why, in theory, Muslim banks are based on different principles, excluding the use of interest.

Elsewhere ...

In Ancient Greece and Rome, in the Jewish culture, debt cancellation is commonplace.

> Indeed, in Ancient Greece, even in Christ's time, debt cancellation was a political act, defined, intelligent, fairly frequent, destined to prevent civil war and re-establish harmony between social classes. In fact, there was a vicious circle in motion, whereby the inequalities between rich and poor grew, so that the only way the poor could survive was by getting in debt to the rich, which led directly to internal enslavement, or to civil war and the destruction of the city. It was not enough to seek the cause of this effect, which would have been fatal for the city, but it had to be eradicated, in order to start anew on a good basis. Debt cancellation was therefore a political commonplace of Greek culture, as it is in Jewish culture. In the Jewish tradition, the Jubilee year is precisely the year of remission of all debts, which occurs every hundred years, leading the majority of the population, who are poor and therefore indebted, to 'jubilate', and freeing the people from the threat of enslavement. *Alain Joxe, L'empire du chaos. Les Républiques face à la domination américaine dans l'après-guerre froide [The Empire of Chaos. The Republics versus American domination in the post-Cold War period]* (trans. VB)

Recent initiatives

The Jubilee 2000 Campaign for the abolition of the debt was set up from 1996 on, in many countries in North and South. It consisted of a vast international campaign for the abolition of the debts of the poor countries, mainly at the instigation of churches from all over the world in Europe, America, Africa, Asia, and by social movements and NGOs. The campaign collected 24 million signatures thanks to an unprecedented mobilization of public opinion.

> There is one sign of God's mercy which is especially necessary today: charity [...] Humankind is confronted with new forms of slavery, more subtle than those which existed in the past [...] Many countries, particularly the poorest, are oppressed by a debt which has taken on such proportions as to render almost impossible its repayment. *Pope Jean-Paul II, Bull of Indiction of the Great Jubilee of the Year 2000* (trans. VB)

In the North, especially in Great Britain and Germany, the request for cancellation concerned the debt of only the poorest countries. In the South, demands were often more radical and aimed at complete cancellation of the Third World debt. The social forces engaged in this combat joined up in November 1999 to form Jubilee South, composed of eighty-five movements from forty-two countries. At the end of 2000, as the Jubilee year drew to a close, the conclusion was as clear as daylight: there had been no debt cancellation to speak of. Nevertheless, the Catholic and Protestant Churches considered that the Jubilee Campaign was over. The big British campaign, Jubilee 2000, was considerably weakened by the withdrawal of the support of the Church leaders. In France, the platform 'Dette et Développement' led by the Comité catholique contre la faim et pour le développement (CCFD; Catholic Committee Against Hunger and For Development) and composed of about thirty trade unions and associations (including CADTM France), took up the theme and has become a special interlocutor with the government authorities. As for Jubilee South, it has decided to carry on the fight for total, immediate and unconditional cancellation of the external public debt of the Third World, just like the CADTM.

Q39 Who owes what to whom?

For several centuries, the domination of the North over the South, as well as the great fortunes of the North, have depended on plundering the resources of the South, the slave trade and colonization. The tons of minerals and riches extracted from Latin America, Asia and Africa since the sixteenth century have never been paid for. The dominant European powers of the time helped themselves using force and for their exclusive profit. In no way were the civilizing and evangelizing missions which served to justify them decided with the local populations' consent, nor did they do them much good. Furthermore, the large-scale pillage was accompanied by the destruction of the local economic and social fabric. The territories of the South did not have the means of developing structures to promote their own development; they just served to provide the mother country or dominant power with easy resources. The Indian textile industry, for example, was destroyed by the British Empire. It is, then, perfectly legitimate to ask for financial reparation for this illegitimate exploitation. There therefore exists a historic debt owed by the wealthy classes of the North to the populations of the South, which must be taken into consideration.

Cultural treasures were also spoliated by the rich countries, especially Western Europe. The subjected peoples of the DCs have thus been deprived of the legacy of their ancestors. The richest pickings of their patrimony are now to be seen in the Louvre (Paris), the British Museum (London), at Tervueren (Brussels) and in the museums of Vienna, Rome, Madrid, Berlin, and New York. When it was not straightforward pillage as such, it is well known that representatives of the colonial powers did not hesitate to undervalue what was found in archaeological digs to enable them to take advantage of the local authorities and get the lion's share. Admirers of the arts, among others, should not forget the scandalous conditions under which objects of high cultural value were obtained.

The considerable deficit in human development in the South (*see* Q2) on one hand, and the grave ecological consequences of the present system for the populations of the indebted countries (*see* Q4 and Q37) on the other, and lastly, the legal, political and economic arguments outlined in this chapter, clearly demonstrate that the present financial debt is odious and that the debt that the ruling classes of the North owe to the South is at once historical, human, cultural, social, moral and ecological.

Nevertheless, most of the governments of the South adopt a singular position. They embrace the neo-liberal logic which is at the origin of the iniquitous system of indebtedness, despite the fact that they are supposed to work for the good of their countries. It is on these grounds that we ask the governments of the South to repudiate the financial debt towards the North, but we consider that they too are accountable for having run up this multi-faceted debt.

Consequently, the populations of the South have a right to demand immediate reparation from the ruling classes of both North and South.

> The external debt of the countries of the South has been repaid several times over. Illegitimate, unjust and fraudulent, the debt functions as an instrument of domination, in the sole service of an international system of usury. Those countries that demand the repayment of the debt are the very ones who exploit the natural resources and traditional knowledge of the South. We ask for its unconditional cancellation and for reparation for the historic, social and environmental debts. *Appeal by the Social Movements, World Social Forum, Porto Alegre, 2002*

Q40 Should there be conditions attached to debt cancellation?

The term 'conditionality' designates the very strong constraints imposed on the DCs by the IMF and the World Bank, by means of structural adjustment programmes. If the system of domination created by the debt is to be ended, there has to be a definitive break with the logic of structural adjustment and its conditionalities.

Certain bodies, through the NGOs, are now proposing to subject debt cancellation to positive conditionalities. Reductions could take place if a democratic process is instigated, if projects promoting human development are set up (building schools, health centres) and so on. However tempting they may appear, such positive conditionalities raise the unavoidable question of who has a right to impose them.

Certain institutions (IMF, World Bank, G8 and even some powerful NGOs of the North) believe themselves imbued with the mission of determining Good and Evil. Depending on local conditions, one might choose an irrigation system or prefer to devote the money to solving other serious problems of human development. In our opinion, it is for the populations concerned and their democratically elected representatives, and them alone, to decide. They must be the only ones to establish development priorities, to choose the projects they will embark upon, to control the use of the funds made available and to be responsible for keeping track of progress. They must have full control of the entire process from start to finish. Some decisions may be made after consulting an NGO or specialized institution able to make a useful contribution at the planning level. Dialogue with movements of North and South may be fruitful, of course. But it is fundamental that decisions concerning the South be made by the South and for the South (unlike the present system where the decisions are made in the North to promote the interests of finance and the multinationals of the North).

It is therefore up to the populations of the DCs to dictate conditions, and no one else. To make sure that this principle of decision by the South and for the South is implemented with complete transparency, it is crucial that the debt should have been cancelled and solid safeguards set up. For populations to be able to influence the decision-making process on the use of the funds, they must be fully and actively involved.

One solution would be to set up national development funds in each country, supplied with the money freed up by the debt cancellation and other measures destined to finance real development (*see* Q43). How such funds would be allocated would be decided by the

---

At Porto Alegre, in Brazil, the participation of the citizens in working out municipal budgets has contributed to re-targeting local expenditure towards the main priorities of human development. During the first seven years of the experiment, the proportion of households with access to the water supply rose from 80 to 98%, and the percentage with access to the sewage system almost doubled (from 46 to 85%). *UNDP, Global Human Development Report, 2002*

---

populations, using a participative process like the one that has been working in Porto Alegre for over twelve years. It is already bearing fruit in the Brazilian town at the cutting edge of this very struggle, and can be adapted by the different DCs liberated from the debt.

Any decisions on major borrowing must be decided by parliament after a vast public debate. This participative democracy, conjoined with the cancellation of the debt and the renunciation of SAPs, is the only way to give back to the peoples of the DCs the power of decision over their lives. The only acceptable conditionalities are those emanating from the populations of the South.

What you do for others without the others, is against the others. *Touareg Proverb, quoted by Daniel Mermet, Agenda 2001* (trans. VB)

NINE

Issues raised by debt cancellation

Q41 If the creditors decided to cancel the debt, would it cause a global financial crisis?

The external public debt of all the DCs taken together, estimated at $1,600 billion, constitutes an unbearable burden for the weak financial capacities of the countries of the South. Yet this debt represents very little indeed by comparison with the enormous indebtedness of the North.

In 2002, the public debt of the Triad came to $20,000 billion (*see*

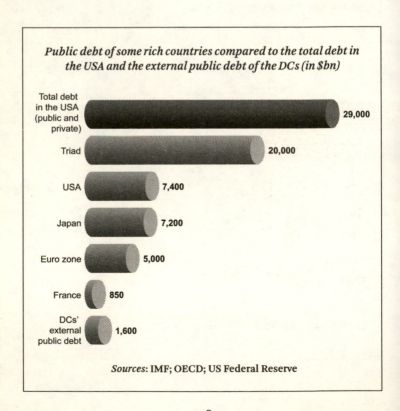

Public debt of some rich countries compared to the total debt in the USA and the external public debt of the DCs (in $bn)

Total debt in the USA (public and private) — 29,000

Triad — 20,000

USA — 7,400

Japan — 7,200

Euro zone — 5,000

France — 850

DCs' external public debt — 1,600

Sources: IMF; OECD; US Federal Reserve

Map 5, page xv), i.e. twelve times the external public debt of the DCs. (Let it be said that we consider that measures should be taken to deal with this public debt, too, which is mainly held by private financial institutions [*see* Q47].)

The total debts of the USA (government debts, household debts and businesses' debts) came to $29,000 billion, i.e. eighteen times the debt we want cancelled. The debts of US businesses alone came to $16,000 billion, while the debts of all the private businesses on the planet came to roughly $30,000 billion.

The external public debt of the DCs is known to account for less than 3 per cent of global lending. In no way would cancelling it endanger the global finance system.

It is interesting to compare the external public debt of a group of DCs with the public debt of certain rich countries that have managed to maintain strong economic links.

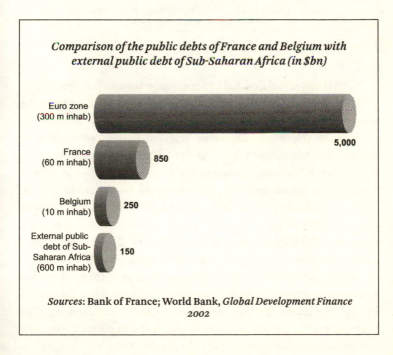

Comparison of the public debts of France and Belgium with external public debt of Sub-Saharan Africa (in $bn)

Euro zone (300 m inhab) — 5,000
France (60 m inhab) — 850
Belgium (10 m inhab) — 250
External public debt of Sub-Saharan Africa (600 m inhab) — 150

Sources: Bank of France; World Bank, *Global Development Finance 2002*

Or again:

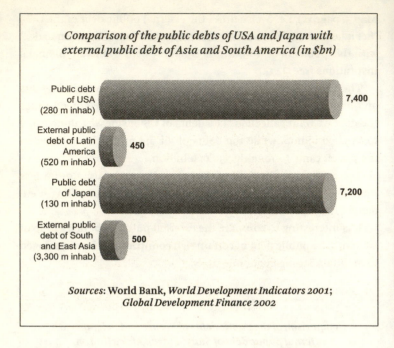

Comparison of the public debts of USA and Japan with external public debt of Asia and South America (in $bn)

Public debt of USA (280 m inhab): 7,400

External public debt of Latin America (520 m inhab): 450

Public debt of Japan (130 m inhab): 7,200

External public debt of South and East Asia (3,300 m inhab): 500

Sources: World Bank, *World Development Indicators 2001*; *Global Development Finance 2002*

Furthermore, the first half of 2002 gave interesting figures that enrich our argument. The telecommunications sector is one of the most heavily indebted in the world, and powerful multinationals like France Telecom or Deutsche Telekom have a very high debt, estimated at $69 billion for the former and $66 billion for the latter, in June 2002. The total is comparable to the external public debt of South Korea, one of the most heavily indebted DCs. In summer 2002, after the revelation of financial malpractice to the tune of $7.2 billion, Worldcom, the second largest US long-distance telephone operator, took refuge from its creditors behind Article 11 of the US Bankruptcy Code (authorizing the firm to pursue its activities without repaying its debts for three months). What about Malaysia, then, which has a comparable external public debt, but could not take refuge from its creditors during the Southeast Asian financial crisis in 1997? The multinationals have become so huge that they can often impose their will on sovereign states.

The creditors of the external public debt of the DCs are not simple

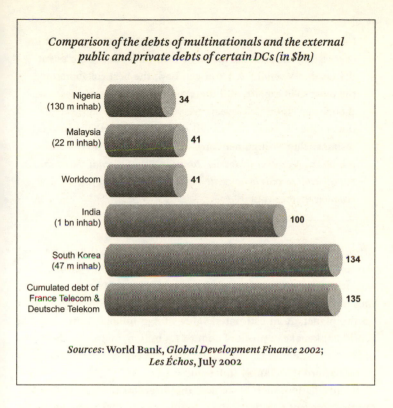

Comparison of the debts of multinationals and the external public and private debts of certain DCs (in $bn)

Nigeria (130 m inhab) — 34
Malaysia (22 m inhab) — 41
Worldcom — 41
India (1 bn inhab) — 100
South Korea (47 m inhab) — 134
Cumulated debt of France Telecom & Deutsche Telekom — 135

Sources: World Bank, *Global Development Finance 2002*; *Les Échos*, July 2002

citizens, they are states, multilateral institutions or big private organizations. Even if it is counted in billions of dollars, the debt of the DCs does not play in the same division as the gigantic sums manipulated by international finance. All the creditors have plenty of other debtors far better off. They have made a lot of money from the debt of the DCs, from privatizations throughout the world, from the neo-liberal offensive against salary-earners and small producers over the last twenty years. They have already been amply repaid for all the sums lent and the risks taken. Now it is time to say, Stop!

The argument that debt cancellation would set a bad example to all present and future borrowers by increasing the moral hazard (*see* Glossary) weighing on loans is hypocritical and erroneous. Hypocritical, because financial markets, where there is permanent speculation, have never been considered paragons of philanthropic virtue.

> I assert the right to earn money. And even a lot of money, if I successfully carry out the missions for which I have been put at the head of Vivendi [...] You can have the best collaborators, the most solid experts, still there are moments when it feels as though the storm will sweep everything away. At those times, the solitude is total. My overall earnings counterbalance this responsibility. No argument anyone can come up with will make me blush. *Jean-Marie Messier, former CEO of Vivendi Universal, Faut-il avoir peur de la nouvelle économie? [Should we fear the new economy?]* (trans. VB)

Erroneous, because the risk is intrinsically linked to the market and not to the personal character of such and such a contractor.

Furthermore, the IMF and the World Bank hold resources that they rarely mention. The IMF has one of the largest holdings of gold on the planet, at an estimated value of $30 billion. Every year, the World Bank makes a profit of about $1.5 billion, mainly on the backs of the DCs. Their refusal to cancel the debt on the pretext that they cannot afford it is frankly indecent.

If cancellation, such as we demand, prevents them from carrying out their present functions, the institutions will disappear. Since the world needs multilateral institutions, they will be replaced by new bodies – this time, truly democratic.

If the IMF and the World Bank devoted all their present funds to organizing the cancellation of the external public debt of the DCs, they could bow out gracefully, having participated at least once to the welfare of humankind. How many more financial crises and human catastrophes do they need before withdrawing humbly from the stage?

The international debt bubble is enormous. A similar bubble burst in Japan at the end of the 1980s, and the Japanese economy has not picked up again since; it is still auditing dubious debts. It is not impossible that the USA, which managed to scrape through in the 1980s and 1990s by getting others to bear the brunt of its deficit and its military operations, will fall foul of the household and business debt crisis as well as the present simmering crisis on the stock exchange and the permanent war it is waging against Third World countries. The cost of rescue there is likely to be far higher than that of cancellation of the DCs' debt. Between the beginning of the fall in stock values in 2000 and summer 2002, over $15,000 billion went up in smoke. That is almost ten times the total external public debt of the DCs.

The cancellation of the external public debt of the DCs involves a sum much too small to cause an international financial crisis. On the other hand, maintaining the debt could very well cause one.

> The rich nations could eliminate the debt of Africa without even noticing it economically. *Jesse Jackson, President of the Rainbow Coalition, USA*

Q42 Could cancelling the debt cause an impoverishment of the North, particularly for tax-payers?

The DCs repay their debts to the states of the North, the multilateral institutions (of which those states are the main shareholders) and private banks in the North. We have shown that wealth goes from the South to the North (with the ruling classes in the South skimming off their commission), despite the generous speeches made in the industrialized countries. Will the North miss this wealth? Will cancelling the debt cause it impoverishment?

First, it is useful to compare the sums at stake with world advertising and military spending, respectively (see page 144). It can only be salutary for humankind to reconsider these outrageous sums.

It should also be pointed out that the creditors have already been repaid several times over by the DCs. For every $1 owed in 1980, the DCs have repaid $7.5 and still owe $4 (*see* Q22). So it is hardly a question of theft if a decision is made to stop! The creditors have already been amply rewarded for the loan of their capital.

As far as private creditors are concerned, their revenues would fall, so the dividends paid out to their shareholders would have to be reduced accordingly, which would primarily affect the better-off

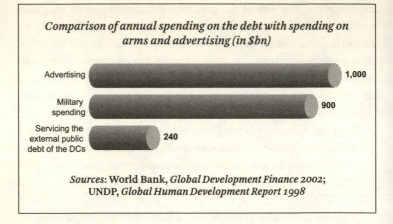

Comparison of annual spending on the debt with spending on arms and advertising (in $bn)

Advertising — 1,000

Military spending — 900

Servicing the external public debt of the DCs — 240

Sources: World Bank, *Global Development Finance 2002*; UNDP, *Global Human Development Report 1998*

classes. Thus private creditors would simply have to erase from their accounts the money coming in from the DCs.

For bilateral creditors, the debt they hold towards the DCs entitles them to a rebate[1] that varies from country to country, but is about 75 per cent of its nominal value. Thus the real value of bilateral credits is less than $150 billion, i.e. a quarter of the total military budgets of the highly industrialized countries ($600 billion of the $900 billion of global spending).

In line with our analysis throughout this book, it is logical to propose that the North should be obliged to pay reparation to the peoples of the DCs, on the grounds of a historic, human, moral, environmental, social and cultural debt. The cancellation of the debt can be the first step, preliminary to reparation.

---

1 The states of the North know that the credits they hold for loans mainly made in the 1970s and 1980s would be worth a lot less than their nominal value were they to be sold on the money markets. That is why the public treasuries of the Paris Club's member countries mark them down significantly. Thus the industrialized countries acknowledge that the value of the external debt is at most 25 per cent of its nominal value. For example, this mark-down is 75 per cent for Vietnam, and over 90 per cent for the Congo Democratic Republic (formerly Zaire). The private part contracted on the money markets is also significantly marked down, as we saw with regard to vulture-funds (*see* Q29). The multilateral part is barely affected, owing to the status of priority lender enjoyed by the Bretton Woods institutions, which are always repaid.

A transfer of technology could also be usefully organized. Why not decide on a lump sum for the inventors of techniques which improve the lives of humankind as a whole, so that they can be placed in the public domain as quickly as possible, and then given to the populations of the South? In the essential domain of medicine, why not decide to make research a public service entirely financed by the government, without patents, and all results going directly into the the public domain, worldwide? There are plenty of possibilities, but the political will is dramatically lacking.

To return to the comparison with slavery, activists who battled against slavery did not stop to ask if the abolition of slavery would deprive the North of resources, or if it would impoverish the rich countries. Fired by an ideal of justice, they already had to take on all those whose primary concerns were profit and wealth. It is true that it is very convenient to be able to import gold, cotton and coffee at low prices because labour is ruthlessly exploited in the South. But we cannot ignore the human cost. After abolition, the North did not suffer from impoverishment; quite the contrary. At least it grew morally richer.

The total cancellation of the external public debt would require little effort in the North, yet it would mean salvation for the South.

We are trying to find a way of making a self-reliant Argentina which does not take money from American plumbers and carpenters who earn 50,000 dollars a year and wonder what their money is being used for. *Paul O'Neill, US Secretary to the Treasury, CNN, 18 August 2001*

The US Treasury Secretary Paul O'Neill has tried to give the impression that it is the American taxpayers, its plumbers and carpenters, who pay for the multi-billion-dollar bail-outs – and because they pay the costs, they ought to have the vote. But that is wrong. The money comes ultimately from workers and taxpayers in the developing countries, for the IMF almost always gets repaid. *Joseph Stiglitz, Globalization and Its Discontents, 2002*

Before we end, let us note that the same procedure is at work in the North. We have seen the impressive amounts of the public debt of the Triad, something in the order of $20,000 billion (even if it is essentially internal). Of course, the repayments it requires are very costly to tax-payers, and profit the private banks and other institutional investors who thus prosper on the backs of the citizens of the North. The mechanism is just as subtle. A growing portion of taxes goes to the repayment of the debt, and, in exchange, the state disengages itself from areas where its role is central (social security, education, culture) and multiplies privatizations. We also need to think about this mechanism of spoliation of the populations of the North by institutional investors accumulating their profits (*see* Q47).

Should the lifestyle of the North not be reconsidered?

According to the UNDP, annual spending on alcoholic drinks in Europe is over $150 billion, and about $50 billion is spent on cigarettes. Global spending related to drug-trafficking comes to about $400 billion, spending on perfume was estimated at $34 billion in 2001. In the circumstances, could the lifestyle of the citizens of the North not be reconsidered, with a view to wasting less and freeing up more resources? Does consuming large quantities of cosmetics and cigarettes matter, while the rest of humanity survives on less than $2 a day? It is time to wake up. Better allocation of resources would enable everyone to live better while at the same time consuming less. Then the cancellation of the debt would be a source of hope for the North, too, leading to hard thinking about a real redistribution of wealth and a great public debate about development and about the quality of life in the North, now and in the future.

Q43 How can alternative funding be found for the development of the DCs?

It is no use expecting the logic of the market to satisfy essential needs. The 2,800 million people living on less than $2 a day do not have enough spending power to interest the markets. Only government policies can guarantee the fulfilment of basic human needs for all. This is why it is necessary for political leaders to allocate political and financial means to honour their commitments to their people.

The application of the Universal Declaration of Human Rights and the International Pact for Economic, Social and Cultural Rights can be obtained only through the concerted action of a powerful social and citizens' movement. The first step is to stop the haemorrhage of resources represented by the repayment of the debt.

Once this first step has been taken, the present economy of international indebtedness must be replaced by a socially just and ecologically sustainable model of development independent of the fluctuations of the financial markets and the loan conditionalities of the IMF and the World Bank.

If cancelling the debt is to serve human development, the money hitherto destined to repay the debt needs to be paid into a development fund controlled democratically by local populations. This development fund, already supplied with money saved through debt cancellation, could be further financed by the following measures.

Give back to the citizens of the DCs what was stolen from them

Considerable wealth, illicitly accumulated by government officials and local capitalists, has been placed securely in the industrialized countries, with the complicity of private financial institutions and the acquiescence of the governments of the North. This movement continues today (*see* Q44).

Restitution requires the completion of judicial procedures conducted both in the Third World and the industrialized countries. A further advantage of such investigations is that the corrupters and the corrupted would no longer get away with their crimes. It is the only hope, if democracy and transparency are ever to overcome corruption.

The resolutions made at the international conference in Dakar in December 2000 ('From Resistance to Alternatives') should also be upheld, demanding reparation for the pillage the Third World has been subjected to for the last five centuries. This implies the restitution of economic and cultural assets stolen from the Asian, African and Latin American continents.

Tax financial transactions

The international platform, ATTAC (in French, Association pour une taxation des transactions financières pour l'aide aux citoyens; Association for the Taxation of Financial Transactions and for Aid to Citizens), argues for the application of a Tobin-type tax (*see* Glossary) of 0.1 per cent which would bring in an estimated $100 billion annually. This money is to be used to fight inequality and to promote education, public health, food security and sustainable development.

Bring Official Development Assistance (ODA) up to at least 0.7 per cent of GDP

ODA has been falling continuously. In 2001, it represented only 0.22 per cent of the GDP of the industrialized countries. Yet the latter have committed themselves on many occasions, within the UN framework, to reach the objective of 0.7 per cent. Present ODA should be multiplied by three to approach the promised amounts. Estimated now at $51 billion by the Organization for Economic Cooperation and Development (OECD) (*see* Glossary), it would then exceed $150 billion a year. The best thing would be for it to be entirely paid in the form of donations. In fact, rather than terms such as 'aid' or 'donation', the most suitable term henceforth is 'reparation'. After all, the idea is to repair the damage caused by centuries of pillage and unfair exchange.

Levy an exceptional tax on the assets of the very wealthy

In its 1995 report, UNCTAD suggested raising a 'one-shot' tax on the assets of the very wealthy. Such a tax, levied worldwide, would free up considerable funds. This 'one-shot' tax (different from recurrent taxes on the estates of the very wealthy, which exist in some parts of the world), could be levied on a national basis. Such an exceptional solidarity tax – of about 10 per cent of the assets of the wealthiest decile of each country – could generate quite considerable resources.

Get rid of Structural Adjustment Programmes

Structural Adjustment Programmes (SAPs), by encouraging the liberalization of the economies of the South, have succeeded in weakening those states. They have made them more dependent on external fluctuations of world markets, and subjected them to conditionalities imposed by the IMF/World Bank tandem, backed up by the governments of the creditor countries grouped in the Paris Club.

The human results of the SAPs are undeniably negative. They must therefore be eradicated and replaced by policies that aim to fulfil basic human needs, giving priority to domestic markets and food security, and seeking out regional and continental complementarity.

Guarantee that strategic sectors which have been privatized be returned to the public domain

Water reserves and distribution, electricity production and distribution, telecommunications, postal services, railways, companies extracting and transforming raw materials, the credit system, certain sectors of education and health – have all systematically been privatized or are in the process of being so. All these must be returned to the public domain.

Adopt partially self-regulating models of development

This type of development requires the creation of politically and economically integrated zones, the emergence of endogenous development models, reinforcement of domestic markets, creation of a local savings bank for local financing. (On the contrary, in 2001, $120 billion were invested abroad by rich Argentinians while their country was suffocating under an external debt of about $150 billion.) It requires the development of education and health, progressive taxation and other mechanisms of redistribution of wealth, diversification of exports, agrarian reform guaranteeing universal access to land for peasants and farmers, urban reform guaranteeing universal access to housing, and so on.

The logic of the present-day global architecture obliges the DCs to provide cheap raw materials and cheap labour to the Triad, which has the capital and the technology. This system has to be replaced by regional economic groupings. Only partially self-regulating development would allow relationships of South–South complementarity to emerge, which is the indispensable condition for economic development of the DCs and, by extension, of the world.

Act upon trade

The historical tendency to downgrade the terms of exchange has to be brought to an end. This means establishing mechanisms that guarantee better remuneration for the basket of products exported on the global market by developing countries.

Concerning agriculture, as the peasant and small farmers' movement, Via Campesina, puts it, the right of each country (or group of countries) to food sovereignty, and especially to self-sufficiency in staples, must be recognized. Furthermore, the rules of global trade must be subordinate to strict environmental, social and cultural criteria. Health, education, water and culture must be removed from the arena of international trade. Public services are basic rights and must therefore be excluded from the General Agreement on Trade in Services (GATS), which envisages total liberalization of public services.

Moreover, the Trade-Related Intellectual Property Rights (TRIPs) agreement must be banned. It prevents countries of the South from freely producing goods (for example, medicines) which could satisfy the needs of their populations.

Adopt better financial discipline

The repeated financial crises of the 1990s have demonstrated that no sustainable development can be attained without strict control of both capital movements and tax evasion. Several measures are therefore needed to make the financial markets fulfil basic human needs: re-regulation of financial markets; control of capital movements; eradication of tax havens and abolition of banking secrecy to fight tax evasion, embezzlement and corruption efficiently; adoption of rules to protect countries which make use of external borrowing.

Ensure the democratic control of the policy of indebtedness

The decision of a state to contract loans and the terms on which they are contracted must be submitted to popular approval (debate and vote in parliament, citizens' control).

Complementary measures are indispensable, beginning with equality between men and women and the rights of indigenous peoples to self-determination.

Q44 Won't the dictatorial regimes currently in office benefit most from debt cancellation?

The total cancellation of the DCs' debt is only the first stage, as we have seen. Once total cancellation has been obtained, the power relations will be reversed. A different logic will then come into play.

Why is it that dictators manage to get into power and stay there for so long? Why does their existence make it so hard for democratic forces to consolidate and break through? Why were dictators like Suharto in Indonesia, Mobutu in Zaire, Omar Bongo in Gabon, Gnassingbe Eyadema in Togo or the Apartheid regime in South Africa able to remain in place for more than thirty years? Why have so many *coups d'état* overthrown democratically elected governments like that of Salvador Allende in Chile or Patrice Lumumba in the former Belgian Congo when it first won independence? To answer the last question: because they tried to break away from the system. The multinationals of the North can get hold of the natural resources of the South more easily under a corrupt and dictatorial government than under a democratic one that demands a better price for its goods. In fact, dictatorships are strengthened by the debt system because they skim off part of the borrowed money to stay in place.

This is why we consider the expropriation of ill-gotten gains indispensable (*see* Q43). There need to be meticulous judicial inquiries on cases of embezzlement and the assets deposited by the moneyed classes of the DCs in tax havens and Northern banks, in order to destabilize existing dictatorships. These assets represent two-thirds of the external public debt of the DCs: $1,100 billion are deposited by the rich of the DCs in the banks of the Triad countries (*see* Map 6, page xvi).

If it is proved that embezzlement has taken place, the expropriation of the ill-gotten gains must be organized, followed by their restitution to the populations from which they were extorted by unscrupulous leaders. Hidden sources of funding will thus be cut off, the war booty of dictators confiscated, and neo-colonial patronage, deprived of its means, will have had its day. This will also be a strong signal to all the democrats in the DCs that the present geopolitical 'logic' has at last been overturned.

Let us take an example. Angola, one of the most promising coun-

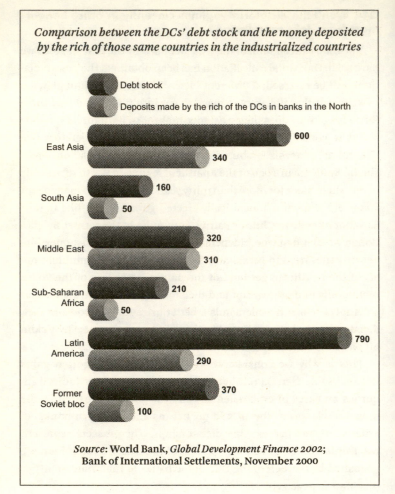

Comparison between the DCs' debt stock and the money deposited by the rich of those same countries in the industrialized countries

Debt stock

Deposits made by the rich of the DCs in banks in the North

East Asia — 600 / 340

South Asia — 160 / 50

Middle East — 320 / 310

Sub-Saharan Africa — 210 / 50

Latin America — 790 / 290

Former Soviet bloc — 370 / 100

Source: World Bank, *Global Development Finance 2002*;
Bank of International Settlements, November 2000

tries for the coming decades in terms of petroleum resources, was ravaged for over twenty-five years by a civil war which ended in 2002 with the death of the leader of one of the two sides (Jonas Savimbi, of UNITA) and a famine which devastated the populations. Elf, the petroleum multinational, helped to arm both camps, as did others, so as to goad the combatants on to ever more ruthless fighting. The two adversaries, UNITA and the government of Eduardo Dos Santos, sold off the oil they had to procure arms. In peacetime, a government which cared about its population would inevitably ask for the renegotiation of the contracts and a re-evaluation of the part reserved for the state. Thus Angola has become heavily indebted and has forfeited its oil to obtain arms.

Indebtedness, corruption and cut-price selling of resources are three aspects of the same problem. Corruption (especially debt-related) is the instrument used to make a leader in power place his country's economy under the 'protection' of the IMF and the US Treasury, of the finance and multinationals of the North, giving them cheap access to natural resources.

What on earth is the matter with these countries where every-thing has to be done for them, where the IMF has to take care of their accounts, NGO missionaries their health and education? Are their leaders incompetent? Yes, and we know why. Because they have been set up by the money-lenders, for the very reason that they are incapable of managing finance other than return-ing it a hundredfold to certain clever devils, helping themselves generously as it goes past. The logical and wholesome solution would be for the debt to be repaid, not by the populations who did not see a penny of it, but first and foremost by all those who took undue advantage of the money: overpaid businesses, grandiose commissions and all their corrupt intermediaries, dictators' war booty, secret funds for political parties. [...] Debt cancellation must be accompanied by international enquiries and legal proceedings to find out what went on, otherwise it would be a reward for delinquency. It is the people's money, and the people must be told what is done with it. *Odile Biyidi, co-founder of the magazine Peuples noirs [Black Peoples] with her late husband the Cameroonian writer Mongo Beti, quoted by François-Xavier Verschave, L'envers de la dette [The wrong side of the debt]* (trans. VB)

In the case of the total cancellation of the DCs' external public debt, the international institutions which decide to do it, whether the present ones or more democratic replacements, will have adopted a new logic and will have managed to impose it upon the various actors. They should have no difficulty, then, in getting national development funds set up for the DCs, democratically run by the populations concerned.

> Staggering under an inflation rate of 44 per cent and an economy in tatters, Turkey has just asked the IMF to bail it out with a loan of $5 billion. In exchange, the IMF has called on Turkey to abolish the death penalty and to respect human rights [...] Nah, just joking! As usual, the IMF is demanding price increases and mass redundancies. *Charlie Hebdo (French weekly), 6 December 2000* (trans. VB)

Whereas the debt has profited dictatorships, cancellation will lead to a fundamental questioning.

Q45 If and when the debt is cancelled, how can a new round of indebtedness be avoided?

The total cancellation of the debt should go along with a change of logic, and new types of funding (*see* Q43). These new sources of money destined to supply the national development funds (to be run by the local populations) do not imply fresh borrowing.

Below, we evaluate the sums involved, point by point:

- After cancellation, the DCs would no longer have to pay debt service. Even if they were to find themselves refused credit access (as creditors could refuse to lend to countries which had obtained total debt cancellation), they would save about $70 billion a year (*see* Q23) which they could redeploy for their domestic needs.
- The expropriation of ill-gotten gains, after the inquiries into embezzlement and corruption among the ruling classes of the South, would funnel considerable sums back to the DCs – in the order of tens of billions of dollars a year for several years.
- Tripling the ODA to 0.7 per cent of the GDP of the rich countries, and paying it exclusively in the form of donations, as reparation

for a historic, human, moral, social, ecological and cultural debt, this time owed to the South, would bring in about $150 billion a year.

- A Tobin-type tax of 0.1 per cent on financial speculation linked to the exchange markets, estimated at $1,200 billion a day in 2001, would bring in at least $100 billion which should go to the DCs.
- A calculated rise in the prices of raw materials and agricultural products, through the concerted action of the producer countries which would no longer be under an obligation to procure hard currency for their repayments, could provide substantial income and at the same time allow a reallocation of land, favouring food crops, reducing the areas cultivated for export produce and better preserving resources, forests and land.
- Redistributive tax policies within the DCs could do away with the inequalities brought about by the dual logic of the debt and structural adjustment. A 'one-shot' tax on the estates of the richest 10 per cent of families in each country would generate substantial fiscal revenues.

All these measures are suitable for financing an 'alternative development' within the context of an 'alternative globalization'. In any case, they limit the need for borrowing.

Q46 Should recourse to borrowing be avoided at all costs?

Our plan of action aims to eradicate usury, but not reasonable recourse to borrowing. This is not unwholesome in itself. Our arguments need to be understood in the context of a meticulous analysis of the present debt crisis.

To prevent a repetition of the present situation of massive over-indebtedness, and the implacable mechanism of domination it represents, recourse to borrowing needs to be limited as far as possible.

We have made proposals for alternative financing (*see* Q43): national and international taxes, encouragement of domestic saving, restitution of ill-gotten gains, increase of ODA in the form of donations as reparation, and so on. If these measures were implemented, the need to borrow would play a much less significant role.

Nevertheless, any decision to contract a major loan should be made under the supervision of the populations concerned, as part of their active management of the national development funds, and debated in parliament (or whatever the legislative body in place), leading up to a transparent vote.

It is also essential that the conditions of the loan should be acceptable, and that the government's signature to contract the loan should not equate to abandoning economic sovereignty and handing the creditors the house-keys, as has too often been the case. Perhaps it would be a good idea to diversify the creditors, so that none can become too pressing. To do that, the present system needs to be reformed. As we have seen, the creditors have taken good care to build multilateral institutions tailored to their needs (IMF, World Bank, Paris Club, London Club) and to take on each debtor alone, thus placing the debtor at their mercy.

Two new principles need to be respected. First, the obligation to repay and to pay interest on these loans, granted at low interest rates, below market conditions, will be valid only if it is proven that the debt did indeed enable the creation of sufficient wealth in the countries concerned.

Second, a strong and efficient protection of debtor countries needs to be organized in favour of the DCs on an international scale, so that those countries can defend themselves against all forms of abuse and spoliation by the banks, international private investors and international financial institutions

Q47 Can the DCs' external public debt be compared to the public debt of the North?

Although the difference in amounts is enormous, the first similarity is in the way they evolve over time. The public debt of the DCs and the public debt of the North both came to a crisis in the 1970s. In the North, the general recession of the years 1973–75 obliged governments to borrow to restart their economic activity: creation of jobs in the public sector, state-sponsored projects (for example, Ariane, Airbus or the Minitel in France), a policy of major industrial or military works. Thus states and local collectivities were ensnared alike by the rise of interest rates at the beginning of the 1980s. Their public debt (mainly internal) grew very fast as they had to take out further loans to repay, as did the South. So here, too, there was a snowballing effect.

The second similarity concerns the credit-holders and the financial flows that they impose. The public debt in the North is largely internal, but the part held by citizens of modest means is marginal. When, in the North, a government puts out a loan offer through Treasury bonds, the big private financial institutions (banks, insurance companies, mutual funds, pension funds) grab almost everything in a few days. Here, too, it is these very well-off individuals who hold the major part of the public debt in the North. The main difference with the DCs resides in the fact that their external public debt obliges them to procure hard currency for their repayments, leading to an over-reliance on exports. From the point of view of the debtors, the state repays using money taken from tax revenues. Now workers' income is more highly taxed than capital income. Furthermore, indirect taxation, such as VAT, tends to increase, which is relatively more costly for the middle and popular classes. Thus the state mainly repays the rich private financial institutions with money raised by heavy taxation of those with modest incomes. Again, there is a transfer of wealth, here all in the North, from the populations to the capital-holders. Thus there are objective grounds for solidarity between the victims of the public debt in the DCs and those of the public debt in the North.

Lastly, a third point of similarity is that in the North, as in the South, heavy indebtedness is the ideal pretext for imposing austerity policies and modifying the social balance in the interests of the capital-holders. Introduced in the 1980s, in parallel with the SAPs in the South, these policies found themselves a general framework in the European Union with the Maastricht Treaty. Priority was given to a stringent reduction of the public deficit, which means rigour and austerity, and in particular privatizations, the overhaul of social security and the pension system, and spending cuts in health and education. In France, it is highly symbolic that, in 2002, the newly elected Raffarin government immediately adopted two typical measures: a 5 per cent income-tax cut (which affects fewer than half of all households) and the start of a programme of privatization of thirteen national companies (including Air France, Electricité de

France, Gaz de France, Credit Lyonnais, Dassault Systèmes, Bull). Thus the economic consequences of the debt for the populations – structural adjustment in the South, austerity in the North – have a great deal in common.

The debt strikes in the North and in the South with frightening and comparable vigour, in its origins, its actual mechanisms, and in its consequences. We would now like to open up a new avenue of thought, one which has received little attention so far. From what has been said, it follows logically that the same solutions should be demanded, i.e. the cancellation of the debt of the citizens of the North towards the great private financial institutions. One way of going about it might be to instigate a 'one-shot' wealth tax (for example, 10 per cent of the estates of the wealthiest 10 per cent of households, as proposed by UNCTAD in 1995). The money raised would be used to repay the debt, which in any case is mainly held by the wealthiest sector. For the citizens of the North, the effect would be considerable as the government, freed of the debt burden, would be able to afford to finance social projects, job creation and so on.

The public debt holdings markets (government bond markets), set up by the main beneficiary countries of financial globalization and then imposed on the other countries (without much trouble, usually) are, in the very words of the IMF, the 'cornerstone' of financial globalization. What this means is that it is quite simply the most solid mechanism instigated by financial liberalization for transferring wealth from certain social classes and strata and from certain countries, to others. Tackling the powerbase of finance implies dismantling these mechanisms and therefore cancelling the public debt – not only that of the poorest countries, but also that of any country whose vital social forces refuse to let their government continue to impose austerity budgets on citizens in the name of repaying the interest on the public debt. *François Chesnais, Tobin or not Tobin?, 1999* (trans. VB)

Q48 How can we achieve cancellation of the DCs' debt and a general improvement of the human condition?

The total cancellation of the external public debt of the DCs could happen in either of two ways.

The first scenario: an initiative on the part of the creditors

Once upon a time ... the creditors did something unheard-of. The IMF and the World Bank, both UN institutions, charged with implementing full employment (as appears in the statutes of the IMF) and the common welfare, draw up a rigorous analysis of structural adjustment and decide to abandon it as it contravenes their mission. At last they reform themselves. This change is made possible only because a new US government has been elected on a progressive programme of major reforms and global democracy. Consequently, the government volunteers to give up its right of veto in the IMF and the World Bank, and, with other countries with the same aspirations, it decides to modify the decision-making process so that the majority of votes go to the countries where the majority of the world's population live.

In the spirit of promoting both sustainable and socially just development on a global scale, the USA also decides to ratify the numerous international treaties pursuing this objective that they have not yet ratified. These are: the International Pact for Economic, Social and Cultural Rights of 1966; the 1979 Convention on the Elimination of All Forms of Discrimination Against Women; the 1989 Convention on the Rights of the Child; the 1948 Convention on the Rights of Organization and Collective Negotiation; the 1949 Convention on Trade Union Freedom and the Protection of Trade Union Rights; the 1951 Convention on Equal Pay; the 1958 Convention on Discrimination in Employment and the Professions; the 1989 Convention on the Status of Refugees; the treaty instigating the International Criminal Court which became effective on 1 July 2002; the Kyoto Protocol of 1997 on the reduction of greenhouse gas emissions (despite its timorous and non-restrictive character, daring to entrust the management of the planet to the laws of the market through the sale of pollution permits); and so on.

Considering the odious character of a large part of the DCs' debts and in recognition of their responsibility in setting off the 1982 debt crisis (by deciding to raise interest rates) and during the period of deregulation encouraged by the IFI, the representatives of the USA, along with those of the other industrialized countries and the indebted countries, decide to cancel all debts owing to the IMF, the World Bank and the regional development banks (African, Asian and Inter-American). They then decide to give these institutions, profoundly reformed and democratized, new means. Moreover, the Triad governments decide that the private financial institutions which hold the credit for the indebted countries and/or have bought up their debt securities must pass the corresponding sums off as profit and loss (the sums represent only a marginal portion of their assets). A fund is set up to provide 100 per cent compensation to small holders of debt securities of the indebted countries.

The governments ask the same private financial institutions to declare on their honour the amounts deposited by dictators (or their beneficiaries), corrupt officials, crooked company managers, organized criminals, and so on. They are led to understand that they should freeze these holdings until thoroughgoing inquiries and criminal procedings can be held. The private institutions are informed that they may be sued and risk heavy fines and prison sentences if they are found to have concealed laundered money or dishonestly obtained fortunes. Furthermore, the judicial authorities and judges have the right to lift banking secrecy and to order sequestration, if the fulfilment of their mission so requires.

After these criminal proceedings, the sums received are transferred to the national development funds of the countries where the money came from. These funds will be managed by the governments of the countries concerned under the active supervision of the citizens' movements and will be used for projects of public utility, devised and elaborated with the direct participation of the citizens concerned, who will have previously defined their priorities.

As for the bilateral debt, the leaders of the rich countries and the other creditor countries decide to erase the debts from their accounts.

More generally, to avoid repeating the financial crises caused by the massive flight of capital and speculative attacks on currencies (there have been several dozen in twenty years), the governments decide to instal a Tobin-type tax and apply Article 6 of the IMF statutes which authorizes (encourages, even) countries to exercise control over capital movements: 'Member-states may take the necessary measures of control to regulate international movements of capital.'

The same governments decide to outlaw tax havens, and companies are forbidden to carry out any operation whatsoever within those territories. They decide to harmonize their policies with their international commitments, especially the promise made at the UN to bring ODA up to 0.7 per cent of their GDP.

They decide to make drastic reductions in arms spending.

They abrogate within the WTO the Trade-Related Intellectual Property Rights (TRIPs) agreement and put an end to the negotiations on the General Agreement on Trade in Services (GATS), which generalize the commercialization of the world.

They decide to place medical research under the responsibility of governments, giving priority to the fight against the most common diseases, such as AIDS and malaria, and making discoveries available to all to encourage the production of generic drugs.

They decide to promote and concretize equality between the sexes.

They set up a global fund for the fulfilment of basic human needs by making over at least $80 billion a year.

The list of progressive measures to be taken is too long to be quoted exhaustively. To get a fuller idea, it is useful to refer to proposals advanced by a series of movements such as the CADTM, ATTAC, Via Campesina, the World March of Women, Jubilee South. There are also the recommendations made by the UN Human Rights Commission, certain reports by UNCTAD, UNDP, UNICEF and the FAO. The measures to be implemented stem of course from the Universal Declaration of Human Rights, the International Pact for Economic, Social and Cultural Rights, and certain UN resolutions such as the one on the right to development.

Clearly, such measures would soon show results:

- our blue planet would breathe more freely
- a sustainable cycle of economic growth would take off, there

would be almost full employment thanks to the general application of the thirty-two-hour week without loss of wages and with compensatory recruitment
- global human welfare would improve significantly faster than the GDP and world trade
- international political tensions would ease
- for the first time in history, a democratic system with citizens' participation would be established on a world scale

It is probable that things will not happen exactly in this way, in which case, the first scenario needs to be revised...

The second scenario: an initiative by the citizens of the debtor countries (and some of their governments) and of the creditor countries

Weary of seeing promises of debt cancellation disappear in a mire of procedure and pretence, revolted by the disastrous effects of structural adjustment programmes, confronted by repeated financial crises, the citizens' movements increase the pressure on both the governments of the indebted countries and those of the creditor countries. As happened in Argentina in December 2001, governments and even presidents have to back down before the clamour of the crowd.

It is no good: the G8, the IMF, the World Bank, the Paris Club and the private financial institutions will not give in. In the USA, the government is still bent on the same course as Reagan, Bush Senior, Clinton and Bush Junior.

It is therefore highly possible that the next weak link in the debt chain to break (it could be Brazil, or Venezuela, but that is not the point), scalded by the Argentine experience and faced with refusal, will radicalize its position regarding the debt and go beyond simply suspending payments, either deciding to repudiate the debt or encouraging the creation of a front of refusal to pay.

The most important thing is that the citizens' movements will have raised awareness and mobilized the population so that suspension or repudiation will be combined with complementary measures leading to a progressive, democratic and socially just solution. Another important thing is that the citizens' movements in the creditor countries should understand the link between the debt and financing development, so as to obtain the maximum number of concessions from the creditors and to support and reinforce the action of their comrades in the indebted countries.

Finally, the positive measures mentioned in the first scenario will probably not be implemented spontaneously by the governments, but as the result of enormous popular pressure. Even more likely, the popular movement will have to find itself leaders as devoted to the cause as Bush, Blair, Schröder, Chirac, Aznar, Koizumi and Berlusconi are to the power of money.

Alas, a third scenario cannot be excluded

The prolongation on a global scale of repeated crises, with very poor growth, even long periods of recession, massive unemployment, increased mortality in the indebted countries, wars, the growth of right-wing extremism. In short, the simple continuation of the present scenario.

It is up to us to act, in the South as well as in the North.

TEN

The international campaign for debt cancellation

Q49 How did the international campaign for the cancellation of the debt start?

The international campaign for the cancellation of the debt is now central to the movement for an alternative globalization. Backed by the biggest petition in history (24 million signatures collected between 1998 and 2000), it unites movements of all kinds, spread over all the continents.

Although the debt issue is not new, it has taken several years to form an international network of such far-reaching proportions.

In the Third World, the campaign for the non-payment of the external debt became massive and popular between 1982 and 1990 in Latin America, the continent most affected by the crisis. Numerous Latin American trade union and peasant farmer organizations tried to promote continental solidarity. Cuba played an active role in trying to federate the Latin American countries in favour of stopping debt repayments.

In the North, certain organizations pioneered the campaign, such as the Association internationale des techniciens, experts et chercheurs (AITEC) (International Association of Technicians, Experts and Researchers) in Paris, which first broached the subject in 1983, or the CADTM in Belgium from 1990 onwards. Several books by Susan George[1] had a considerable influence in reinforcing the movement in its early stages.

The international campaign found new fervour in the late 1990s, with the launch of the Jubilee 2000 campaign (with the support of the Catholic and Protestant Churches). In May 1998, at the G8 summit in Birmingham (UK), 70,000 Britons demonstrated for the cancellation

---

1 George, Susan, *A Fate Worse than Debt* (London: Penguin Books, 1988); *The Debt Boomerang: How Third World Debt Harms Us All* (Boulder, CO: Westview Press 1992). Susan George is Vice-President of ATTAC France.

of the debt of the poor countries under the banner of Jubilee 2000 Great Britain.

Jubilee South was launched in Johannesburg in 1999. Its headquarters are in the Philippines and it includes organizations from all the continents of the South (Asia, Africa, Latin America), co-ordinated by country and by continent.

Other networks have been founded in several countries in the North, especially France with the Dette et Développement (Debt and Development) campaign, which includes NGOs, trade unions and associations like the CADTM France and the Comité catholique contre la faim et pour le développement (CCFD; Catholic Committe against Hunger and for Development). In Spain, in 1999, the Citizens' Network for the Abolition of the External Debt (RCADE) was founded and organized a referendum for the cancellation of the debt in which over a million people voted, on 12 March 2000.

Several networks have accomplished the task of systematic convergence. Debates run through the movement: should cancellation be unconditional, or not? Jubilee South, the CADTM and the RCADE think it should; several Jubilee 2000 campaigns in countries of the North (especially Great Britain and Germany) and some in the South (Peru, for example) are in favour of conditionalities. Other subjects for debate are: should we follow the new strategy of the IMF and the World Bank with a critical eye, or oppose it? Should the debt be cancelled for all the countries of the Third World or only some of them (the poorest)?

From 1999 onwards, the movements in the South began to grow gradually stronger. Large mobilizations took place in Peru (1999), Ecuador (1999–2001), Brazil (September 2000) and South Africa (1999–2000).

The campaign is not limited to networks dealing specifically with the question of the debt. There is constant synergy with networks active on issues related to the financial markets, the IFI or the WTO. For example, the cancellation of the Third World debt is one of the central demands of the international platform of ATTAC. Organizations like '50 Years is Enough' (USA), the Bretton Woods Project (Great Britain) or Agir Ici (France) are in favour of the cancellation of the debt, since the IMF/World Bank's adjustment plans which they are fighting are the solutions these institutions propose for the over-indebtedness of the DCs. The international peasant farmers' movement, Via Campesina (70 million peasant farmer members, with its HQ in Honduras) also fights against the debt. The World March of Women has taken up the cry. The international trade union federations, CISL and CMT, have given their support. Lastly, networks active in international trade, such as Focus on the Global South, also call for the cancellation of the debt, in so far as it is used by the creditors as a means of blackmailing the debtor countries into opening up their economies to the maximum.

Q50 How was the CADTM founded?

Seeing the ravages of neo-liberal corporate-driven policies in the 1980s, more and more citizens identified the debt as the main instrument of subordination of the South. In France, when the G7 met in July 1989, at the time of the bicentenary of the French Revolution, a campaign called Ça suffa comme ci (Enough's enough*)*, launched under the impetus of the writer Gilles Perrault and the singer Renaud, ended by drawing up l'Appel de La Bastille (the Bastille Appeal), demanding immediate and unconditional cancellation of the Third World debt. Although there was no immediate follow-up in France, the campaign was carried on in Belgium, with the founding of the Committee for the Abolition of the Third World Debt (Comité pour l'annulation de la dette du Tiers-Monde or CADTM).

The international network based in Brussels promotes radical alternatives to the different forms of oppression in the world. Third World debt and structural adjustment are at the heart of its preoccupations, to put an end to the dictates of the G8, the transnational firms and the World Bank/IMF/WTO trio. Working in an internationalist perspective, the CADTM is of its essence pluralist. It attracts activists, trade union organizations, political parties, parliamentarians, solidarity campaign committees, NGOs. The ball is rolling ...

The first major turn of events came in 1994. On 1 January, in the Chiapas region of Mexico, the Zapatistas and the Deputy Commander Marcos caused a stir at the time of the implementation of the North American Free Trade Agreement (NAFTA) between Canada, the USA and Mexico. Based on the claims of the indigenous peoples, their opposition also found its place within the general context of the battle against all oppression in the world and against corporate-driven globalization. Nineteen ninety-four also marked the fiftieth anniversary of the Bretton Woods institutions (IMF, World Bank) which was being commemorated in Madrid. On this occasion, the CADTM took part in the campaign Les Autres Voix de la Planète (The Planet's Other Voices) which organized a counter-summit and a street demonstration (15,000 demonstrators) destined to draw attention to an alternative point of view. The campaign gave its name to the CADTM's journal, published every three months.

Next, the petition *Banque mondiale, FMI, OMC: ça suffit* (World Bank, IMF, WTO: enough!) launched by CADTM brought to light a broad network of sympathizers opposed to the international financial institutions' logic. In 1996 the G7 summit in Lyon was the scene of huge international mobilization, still using the theme 'The Planet's Other Voices', followed by the 'Intergalactic Meeting of Zapatistas' in La Realidad (Mexico).

In 1998, the Jubilee 2000 campaign on the one hand and the birth of ATTAC on the other relaunched the theme of the debt in France and, more generally, in Europe. The CADTM has been working on it from the outset.

Initiatives continued: in 1998 there was Action mondiale des Peuples (People's Global Action) in Geneva and the G8 summit in Birmingham; in 1999, the Jubilee 2000 campaign launched by the churches and the June meetings in Saint-Denis (Paris). After the failure of the WTO summit in Seattle (USA), the movement began to gather momentum, with meetings in Bangkok in February 2000, Geneva in June 2000 and Prague in September 2000.

There have been four major international events organized in the South with the active participation of the CADTM: a North–South Meeting in Dakar in December 2000, and three meetings of the World Social Forum in Porto Alegre (Brazil) in January 2001, February 2002 and January 2003, with, among other events, the International Peoples' Tribunal Against the Debt.

Meanwhile, the CADTM is broadening its field of action:

- an international meeting every two years in Belgium gathering between 600 and 1,400 people

- publications on the debt issue issue like *Your Money or Your Life! The Tyranny of Global Finance* (London: Pluto Press, 1999)
- a continuous spate of lectures (reaching up to 12,000 people a year)
- a certain amount of press coverage, allowing us to reach several million people
- a variety of consciousness-raising actions, for example popular theatre with the Senegalese troop Baamtare who toured Europe in 1997 at the invitation of the CADTM

The CADTM network is growing both in the North (Belgium, Switzerland, France) and in the South (particularly West and Central Africa and the Maghreb). These networks meet up at seminars organized by the CADTM (as in Amsterdam in April 2000 or Brussels in May 2001 and September 2002), at international conferences (Bangkok and Geneva in 2000, Dakar in December 2000, Genoa in July 2001, Liège in September 2001 or again Porto Alegre) or at demonstrations (especially at the G7 summits and the annual general meetings of the IFI).

The CADTM does not limit its actions to the central demand of total and unconditional cancellation of the external public debt of the DCs and the abolition of the SAPs imposed on Third World countries. It also puts forward numerous proposals for constructing sustainable alternatives to the present financial logic, which appear throughout this book.

As a recognized authority on the debt issue and a popular movement mobilizing in both North and South, the CADTM is well equipped to bring its influence to bear on the struggle to construct another world.

Contacts

CADTM Belgique, 345 rue de l'Observatoire, 4000 Liège < belgique@ cadtm.org>

CADTM France, 17 rue de la Bate, 45150 Jargeau < france@cadtm. org>

CADTM Suisse, Case postale 1135, 1211 Genève 1 <suisse@cadtm. org>

For all other countries:

CADTM, 1 rue des Jasmins, 4000 Liège, Belgium <international@cadtm. org>; website: <www.cadtm.org>

Appendix: Lists of countries

165 DCs (authors' count)

East Asia and the Pacific

Brunei, China, East Timor, Fiji, Indonesia, Kampuchea, Kiribati, Laos, Malaysia, Marshall Islands, Micronesia (Federal States), Mongolia, Myanmar, Nauru, North Korea, Palau, Papua New Guinea, Philippines, Solomon Islands, Samoa, Singapore, South Korea, Thailand, Tonga, Tuvalu, Vanuatu, Vietnam.

Latin America and the Caribbean

Antigua and Barbuda, Argentina, Bahamas, Barbados, Belize, Bolivia, Brazil, Chile, Colombia, Costa Rica, Cuba, Dominica, Dominican Republic, Ecuador, Grenada, Guatemala, Guyana, Haiti, Honduras, Jamaica, Mexico, Nicaragua, Panama, Paraguay, Peru, St Kitts and Nevis, St Lucia, St Vincent and Grenadines, Salvador, Surinam, Trinidad and Tobago, Uruguay, Venezuela.

Middle East and North Africa

Algeria, Bahrain, Cyprus, Djibouti, Egypt, Iran, Iraq, Israel, Jordan, Kuwait, Lebanon, Libya, Malta, Morocco, Oman, Qatar, Saudi Arabia, Syria, Tunisia, Turkey, United Arab Emirates, Yemen, Zones under Palestinian administration.

South Asia

Afghanistan, Bangladesh, Bhutan, India, the Maldives, Nepal, Pakistan, Sri Lanka.

Sub-Saharan Africa

Angola, Benin, Botswana, Burkina Faso, Burundi, Cameroon, Cap Verde, Central African Republic, Chad, Comoro Islands, Congo, Democratic Republic of Congo, Equatorial Guinea, Eritrea, Ethiopia, Gabon, Gambia, Ghana, Guinea, Guinea-Bissau, Ivory Coast, Kenya, Lesotho, Liberia, Madagascar, Malawi, Mali, Mauritania, Mauritius, Mozambique, Namibia, Niger, Nigeria, Rwanda, São Tomé and Príncipe, Senegal, Seychelles, Sierra Leone, Somalia, South Africa, Sudan, Swaziland, Tanzania, Togo, Uganda, Zambia, Zimbabwe.

The former Soviet Bloc

Albania, Armenia, Azerbaijan, Byelorussia, Bosnia Herzegovina, Bulgaria, Croatia, Czech Republic, Estonia, Georgia, Hungary, Kazakhstan, Kirghizia, Latvia, Lithuania, Macedonia, Moldavia, Poland, Romania, Russia, Slovakia, Slovenia, Tajikistan, Turkmenistan, Ukraine, Uzbekistan, Yugoslavia.

Triad

Andorra, Australia, Austria, Belgium, Canada, Denmark, Finland, France, Germany, Greece, Iceland, Ireland, Italy, Japan, Liechtenstein, Luxembourg, Monaco, the Netherlands, New Zealand, Norway, Portugal, Spain, Sweden, Switzerland, United Kingdom, United States of America.

42 HIPCs

Angola, Benin, Bolivia, Burkina Faso, Burundi, Cameroon, Central African Republic, Chad, Comoro Islands, Congo, Democratic Republic of Congo, Ethiopia, Gambia, Ghana, Guinea, Guinea-Bissau, Guyana, Honduras, Ivory Coast, Kenya, Laos, Liberia, Madagascar, Malawi, Mali, Mauritania, Mozambique, Myanmar, Nicaragua, Niger, Rwanda, São Tomé and Príncipe, Senegal, Sierra Leone, Somalia, Sudan, Tanzania, Togo, Uganda, Vietnam, Yemen, Zambia.

26 HIPCs having reached the decision point in August 2002

Benin, Bolivia, Burkina Faso, Cameroon, Chad, Ethiopia, Gambia, Ghana, Guinea, Guinea-Bissau, Guyana, Honduras, Madagascar, Malawi, Mali, Mauritania, Mozambique, Nicaragua, Niger, Rwanda, São Tomé and Príncipe, Senegal, Sierra Leone, Tanzania, Uganda, Zambia.

Glossary

Balance of payments

A country's balance of current payments is the result of its commercial transactions (i.e. imported and exported goods and services) and of its financial exchanges with foreign countries. The balance of payments is a measure of the financial position of a country as regards the rest of the world. A country with a surplus in its current payments is a lending country for the rest of the world. On the other hand, if a country's balance is in the red, that country will have to turn to international lenders to borrow the funding it needs.

Central Bank

A country's Central Bank runs its monetary policy and holds the monopoly on minting the national currency. Commercial banks must get their currency from it, at a supply price fixed according to the main rates of the Central Bank.

DCs

The developing countries (*see* Q1).

Debt rescheduling

Modification of the terms of a debt, for example by modifying the due-dates or by postponing repayments of the principal and/or the interest. The aim is usually to give a little breathing space to a country in difficulty by extending the period of repayment and reducing the amount of each instalment or by granting a period of grace during which no repayments will be made.

Debt service

The sum of the interests and the amortization of the capital borrowed.

Debt stock

The total amount of debt.

Devaluation

A lowering of the exchange rate of one currency as regards others.

Export Credit Agency

When private businesses of the North obtain a market in a DC, there is a risk that economic or political problems may prevent payment of bills. To protect themselves, they can take out insurance with an Export Credit Agency such as COFACE in France or Ducroire in Belgium. If there is a problem, the agency pays instead of the insolvent client and the Northern business is sure of getting what is owed.

According to the Jakarta Agreement for the reform of public export credit and credit-insurance agencies, they are 'now the greatest source of public funding in the world, underwriting 8 per cent of global exports in 1998, i.e. 391 billion dollars of investment, mainly for big civil and military projects in the developing countries. It is far more than the annual average of Official Development Assistance [...] which approaches 50 billion dollars. The outstanding debt of the Export Credit Agencies represents 24 per cent of the debt of developing countries and 56 per cent of public credits held on these countries.'

One of the main criticisms lodged against them is that they are not very fussy about the nature of the contracts insured (arms, infrastructure and huge energy projects such as the gigantic Three Gorges Dam project in China) nor about their social or environmental consequences. They often give their support to repressive and corrupt regimes (such as to Total in Myanmar, formerly Burma) which means implicitly supporting fundamental human rights violations.

G8

Group composed of the most powerful countries of the planet: Canada, France, Germany, Italy, Japan, the UK and the USA, with Russia a full member since June 2002. Their heads of state meet annually, usually in June or July.

Genetically modified organisms (GMOs)

Living organisms (plant or animal) which have undergone genetic manipulation in order to modify their characteristics, usually to make them resistant to a herbicide or pesticide. In 2000, GMOs were planted over more than 40 million hectares, three-quarters of that being soybeans and maize. The main countries involved in this production are the USA, Argentina and Canada. Genetically modified plants are usually produced intensively for cattle fodder for the rich countries. Their existence raises three problems.

- The health problem. Apart from the presence of new genes whose effects are not always known, resistance to a herbicide implies that the producer will be increasing use of the herbicide. GMO products (especially American soybeans) end up gorged with herbicide whose effects on human health are not known. Furthermore, to incorporate a new gene, it is associated with an antibiotic-resistant gene. Healthy cells are heavily exposed to the herbicide and the whole is cultivated in a solution with this antibiotic so that only the modified cells are conserved.

- The legal problem. GMOs are being developed only on the initiative of big agri-business transnationals like Monsanto, who are after the royalties on related patents. They thrust aggressively forward, forcing their way through legislation that is inadequate to deal with these new issues. Farmers then become dependent on these firms. States protect themselves as best they can, but often go along with the firms, and are completely at a loss when seed thought not to have been tampered with is found to contain GMOs. Thus, genetically modified rape seed was destroyed in the north of France in May 2000 (Advanta Seeds). Genetically modified maize on 2,600 hectares in the southern French department of Lot et Garonne was not destroyed in June 2000 (Golden Harvest). Taco Bell corn biscuits were withdrawn from distribution in the USA in October 2000 (Aventis). Furthermore, when the European Parliament voted on the recommendation of 12 April 2000, an amendment outlining the producers' responsibilities was rejected.

- The food problem. GMOs are not needed in the North where there is already a problem of over-production and where a more wholesome, environmentally friendly agriculture needs to be promoted. They are also useless to the South, which cannot afford such expensive seed and the pesticides that go with it, and where it could completely disrupt traditional production. It is clear, as is borne out by the FAO, that hunger in the world is not due to insufficient production.

Gross Domestic Product (GDP)

The GDP represents the total wealth produced in a given territory, calculated as the sum of added values.

Gross National Product (GNP)

The GNP represents the wealth produced by a nation, as opposed to a given territory. It includes the revenue of citizens of the nation living abroad.

Heavily Indebted Poor Countries (HIPCs)

See Q25

Human Development Rating (HDR)

This instrument is used by the UN to estimate a country's degree of development, based on per capita income, the level of education and the average life expectancy of the population.

Human Poverty Index (HPI)

Since 1997, the annual UNDP Report tries to measure poverty in the Third World using a human poverty index that considers criteria other than monetary income. These are:

- the probability at birth of not attaining forty years of age
- the percentage of illiterate adults
- services procured by the economy overall. The quality of these is determined using two elements: the percentage of individuals without access to piped drinking water, and the percentage of children under five who are underweight

Despite undeniable monetary poverty, some countries manage to attenuate the impact of that poverty by access to services made available to the population. At the top of the list of such countries in 2002, were Uruguay, Costa Rica, Chile and Cuba. These countries had managed to reduce human poverty to an HPI below 5 per cent.

IMF

International Monetary Fund. *See* Q12. Website: <www.imf.org>

Inflation

The cumulated rise of prices as a whole (e.g. a rise in the price of petroleum, eventually leading to a rise in salaries, then to the rise of other prices). Inflation implies a fall in the value of money since, as time goes by, larger sums are required to purchase particular items. This is the reason why corporate-driven policies seek to keep inflation down.

Interest rates

When A lends money to B, B repays the amount lent by A (the capital) as well as a supplementary sum known as interest, so that A has an interest in agreeing to this financial operation. The interest is determined by the interest rate, which may be high or low. To take a very simple example: if A borrows $100 million for ten years at a fixed interest rate of 5 per cent, the first year he will repay a tenth of the capital initially borrowed ($10 million) plus 5 per cent of the capital owed, i.e. $5 million, that is a total of $15 million. In the second year, he will again repay 10 per cent of the capital borrowed, but the 5 per cent now only applies to the remaining $90 million still due, i.e. $4.5 million, or a total of $14.5 million. And so on, until the tenth year when he will repay the last $10 million, plus 5 per cent of that remaining $10 million, i.e. $0.5 million, giving a total of $10.5 million. Over ten years, the total amount repaid will come to $127.5 million. The repayment of the capital is not usually made in equal instalments. In the initial years, the repayment concerns mainly the interest, and the proportion of capital repaid increases over the years. In this case, if repayments are stopped, the capital still due is higher.

The nominal interest rate is the rate at which the loan is contracted. The real interest rate is the nominal rate reduced by the rate of inflation.

Least Developed Countries (LDCs)

A notion defined by the UN on the following criteria: low per capita income, poor human resources and little diversification in the economy. The list includes forty-nine countries at present, the most recent addition being Senegal in July 2000. Thirty years ago there were only twenty-five LDCs.

The London Club

The members are the private banks that lend to Third World states and companies.

During the 1970s, deposit banks had become the main source of credit for countries in difficulty. By the end of the decade, these countries were receiving over 50 per cent of total credit allocated, from all lenders combined. At the time of the debt crisis in 1982, the London Club had an interest in working with the IMF to manage the crisis.

The groups of deposit banks meet to co-ordinate debt rescheduling for borrower countries. Such groups are known as advisory commissions. The meetings, unlike those of the Paris Club that always meets in Paris, are held in New York, London, Paris, Frankfurt or elsewhere at the convenience of the country concerned and the banks. The advisory commissions, which started in the 1980s, have always advised debtor countries immediately to adopt a policy of stabilization and to ask for IMF support before applying for rescheduling or fresh loans from the deposit banks. Only on rare occasions do commissions pass a project without IMF approval, if the banks are convinced that the country's policies are adequate.

The Marshall Plan

A programme of economic reconstruction proposed in 1947 by the US Secretary of State, George C. Marshall. With a budget of $12.5 billion of the time (about $80 billion in 2002 terms) composed of donations and long-term loans, the Marshall Plan enabled sixteen countries (particularly France, the UK, Italy and the Scandinavian countries) to finance their reconstruction after the Second World War.

Monoculture

When one crop alone is cultivated. Many countries of the South have been induced to specialize in the production of a commodity for export (cotton, coffee, cocoa, groundnuts, tobacco) to procure hard currency for debt repayments.

Moral hazard

An argument often used by opponents of debt cancellation. It is based on the liberal theory which considers a situation where there is a borrower and a lender as a case of asymmetrical information. Only the borrower knows whether he really intends to repay the lender. By cancelling the debt today, there would be a risk that the same facility might be extended to other debtors in future, which would increase the reticence of creditors to commit capital. They would have no other solution than to demand a higher interest rate including a risk premium. Clearly the term 'moral', here, is applied only to the creditors and the debtors are automatically suspected of 'amorality'. Yet it is easily demonstrated that this 'moral hazard' is a direct result of the total liberty of capital flows. It is proportionate to the opening of financial markets, as this is what multiplies the potentiality of the market contracts that are supposed to increase the welfare of humankind but actually bring an increase in risky contracts. So financiers would like to multiply the opportunities to make money without risk in a society which, we are unceasingly told, is and has to be a high-risk society ... a fine contradiction.

Mutual fund

Collective investment fund in the USA, equivalent to SICAV in France.

North Atlantic Treaty Organization (NATO)

NATO ensures US military protection for the Europeans in case of aggression, but above all it gives the USA supremacy over the Western Bloc. Western European countries agreed to place their armed forces within a defence system under US command, and thus recognize the preponderance of the USA. NATO was founded in 1949 in Washington, but became less prominent after the end of the Cold War. In 2002, it had nineteen members: Belgium, Canada, Denmark, France, Iceland, Italy, Luxembourg, the Netherlands, Norway, Portugal, the UK, the USA, to which were added Greece and Turkey in 1952, the Federal Republic of Germany in 1955 (replaced by Unified Germany in 1990), Spain in 1982, Hungary, Poland and the Czech Republic in 1999.

Net transfers on debt

This refers to the subtraction of debt-servicing (yearly payments – interest + capital sum – to the industrialized countries) from the year's gross payments (donations and new loans) made by the creditors.

The net transfer on debt is said to be positive when the country or continent concerned receives more (in loans) than it repays. It is negative if the sums repaid are greater than the sums lent to the country or continent concerned.

OECD (Organization for Economic Co-operation and Development)

The OECD includes the fifteen members of the European Union plus Switzerland, Norway, Iceland; in North America: the USA and Canada; and in Asia and the Pacific: Japan, Australia and New Zealand. Between 1994 and 1996, three Third World countries entered the OECD: Turkey, also a candidate for the EU; Mexico, also part of ALENA with its two North American neighbours; and South Korea (December 1996). Since 1995, three countries of the former Eastern Bloc have joined: the Czech Republic, Poland and Hungary. In 2000, the Slovak Republic became the thirtieth member.

OECD member countries in 2002 in alphabetical order: Australia, Austria, Belgium, Canada, Czech Republic, Denmark, Finland, France, Germany, Greece, Hungary, Iceland, Ireland, Italy, Japan, Luxembourg, Mexico, Netherlands, New Zealand, Norway, Poland, Portugal, Slovakia, South Korea, Spain, Sweden, Switzerland, Turkey, UK, USA. Website: <www.oecd.org>

Official Development Assistance (ODA)

Official Development Assistance is the name given to loans granted in financially favourable conditions by the public bodies of the industrialized countries. A loan has only to be agreed at a lower rate of interest than going market rates (a concessionary loan) to be considered as aid, even if it is then repaid to the last cent by the borrowing country. Tied bilateral loans (which oblige the borrowing country to buy products or services from the lending country) and debt cancellation are also counted as part of ODA. Apart from food aid, there are three main ways of using these funds: rural development, infrastructure and non-project aid (financing budget deficits or the balance of payments). The latter increases continually. This aid is made 'conditional' upon reduction of the public deficit, privatization, environmental 'good behaviour', care of the very poor, democratization and so on. These conditions are laid down by the main governments of the North, the World Bank and the IMF. The aid goes through three channels: multilateral aid, bilateral aid and the NGOs.

Organization of Petroleum-Exporting Countries (OPEC)

OPEP is a group of eleven DCs which produce petroleum: Algeria, Indonesia, Iran, Iraq, Kuwait, Libya, Nigeria, Qatar, Saudi Arabia, United Arab Emirates, Venezuela. These eleven countries represent 41 per cent of oil production in the world and own more than 75 per cent of known reserves. Founded in September 1960 and based in Vienna (Austria), OPEC is in charge of co-ordinating and unifying the petroleum-related policies of its members, with the aim of guaranteeing them all stable revenues. To this end, production is organized on a quota system. Each country, represented by its Minister of Energy and Petroleum, takes a turn in running the organization. Since 1 July 2002, the Venezuelan Alvaro Silva-Calderon has been the Secretary General of OPEC.

Paris Club (Club de Paris)

This group of lender states was founded in 1956 and specializes in dealing with non-payment by developing countries. Website:<www.clubdeparis.org>

Pension funds

Pension funds collect part of their clients' monthly salary and speculate on the financial markets to lay out this capital to advantage. There is a dual objective: first, to provide a pension for their clients when they retire at the end of their working lives; and second, to make extra profits for themselves. Both objectives depend on contingencies and their fulfilment is uncertain. On many occasions, workers have found themselves with neither savings nor a pension after crashing bankruptcies, such as that of the Robert Maxwell business empire in the United Kingdom. The system of pensions by capitalization has become generalized in the Anglo-Saxon world. In 2002, some countries in continental Europe, such as France, still retained a distributive pension-system based on solidarity between generations.

Poverty Reduction Strategy Paper (PRSP)

Set up by the World Bank and the IMF in 1999, the PRSP was officially designed to fight poverty. In fact, it turns out to be an even more virulent version of the SAPs in disguise, to try and win the approval and legitimation of the social participants.

Risk premium

When loans are granted, the creditors take account of the economic situation of the debtor country in fixing the interest rate. If there seems to be a risk that the debtor country may not be able to honour its repayments, then that will lead to an increase in the rates it will be charged. Thus the creditors receive more interest, which is supposed to compensate for the risk taken in granting the loan. This means that the cost to the borrower country is much higher, increasing the financial pressure it has to bear. For example, in 2002, Argentina was faced with risk premiums of more than 4,000 points, meaning that for a hypothetical market interest rate of 5 per cent, Argentina would have to borrow at a rate of 45 per cent. This cuts it off de facto from access to credit, forcing it even deeper into crisis. For Brazil in August 2002, the risk premium was at 2,500 points.

Staples

Crops destined to feed local populations (millet, manioc, etc.), as opposed to cash crops, destined for export (coffee, cocoa, tea, groundnuts, sugar, etc.).

Structural Adjustment

Economic policies imposed by the IMF in exchange for new loans or the rescheduling of old loans (see Q15 and Q16).

Tobin Tax

A tax on exchange transactions (all transactions involving conversion of currency), originally proposed in 1972 by the US economist James Tobin, as a means of stabilizing the international financial system. The idea was taken up by the association ATTAC and other movements for an alternative globalization, including the CADTM. Their aim is to reduce financial speculation (which was of the order of $1,500 billion a day in 2002) and redistribute the money raised by this tax to those who need it most. International speculators who spend their time changing dollars for yens, then for euros, then dollars again, etc., as they calculate which currency will appreciate and which depreciate, will have to pay a small tax, somewhere between 0.1 per cent and 1 per cent, on each transaction. According to ATTAC, this could raise $100 billion on a global scale. Considered unrealistic by the ruling classes to justify their refusal to adopt it, the meticulous analyses of globalized finance carried out by ATTAC and others has, on the contrary, demonstrated how simple and appropriate such a tax would be.

Trade balance

The trade balance of a country is the difference between merchandise sold (exports) and merchandise bought (imports). The resulting trade balance either shows a deficit or is in credit.

UNCTAD (United Nations Conference on Trade and Development)

This was established in 1964, after pressure from the developing countries, to offset the GATT effects. Website: <www.unctad.org>

United Nations Development Programme (UNDP)

The UNDP, founded in 1965 and based in New York, is the UN's main agency of technical assistance. It helps the DCs, without any political restrictions, to set up basic administrative and technical services, trains managerial staff, tries to respond to some of the essential needs of populations, takes the initiative in regional co-operation programmes and co-ordinates, theoretically at least, the local activities of all the UN operations. The UNDP generally relies on Western expertise and techniques, but a third of its contingent of experts come from the Third World. The UNDP publishes an annual Human Development Report which, among other things, classifies countries by their Human Development Rating (HDR; *see* Q2). Website:<www.undp.org>

Warsaw Pact

A military pact between the countries of the former Soviet Bloc (USSR, Albania, Bulgaria, Hungary, Poland, the German Democratic Republic, Romania, Czechoslovakia). It was signed in Warsaw in May 1955, as a reaction to the Federal German Republic joining NATO. Albania withdrew in 1968 after Soviet intervention in Czechoslovakia. After the dislocation of the USSR, the Pact's military organization was dissolved in April 1991.

World Bank

See Q13. Website: <www.worldbank.org>

World Trade Organization (WTO)

The WTO, founded on 1 January 1995, replaced the General Agreement on Trade and Tariffs (GATT). The main innovation is that the WTO enjoys the status of an international organization. Its role is to ensure that no member-states adopt any kind of protectionism whatsoever, in order to accelerate the liberalization of global trading and to facilitate the strategies of the multinationals. It has an international court (the Dispute Settlement Body) which judges any alleged violations of its founding text drawn up in Marrakesh. Website: <www.wto.org>

Bibliography

Chesnais, François, *Tobin or not Tobin (in French)* L'esprit frappeur, 1999

CONGAD, *Nous ne devons rien!, De 'Dakar 2000: Afrique, des résistances aux alternatives' au Forum des Peuples à Siby (Mali)*, 2002

Dette & Développement, *Rapport 2001–2002: La dette des pays du Sud et le financement du développement*, 2002 <www.dette2000.org>

IMF, *World Economic Outlook 2002*

IMF and AID, *HIPC Initiative: Status of Implementation* <www.imf.org>, April 2002

George, Susan and Fabrizio Sabelli, *Crédits sans frontières*, La Découverte, 1994

Harribey, Jean-Marie, *La démence sénile du capital*, du Passant, 2002

Horman, Denis, *La mondialisation excluante*, L'Harmattan, 2001

Millet, Damien, *La tragédie de la dette: d'un colonialisme à un autre*, 2001 <www.ornitho.org>

Norel, Philippe and Éric Saint-Alary, *L'endettement du Tiers-Monde*, Syros, 1992

Ruiz Diaz, Hugo, *La dette extérieure: mécanismes juridiques de non-paiement, moratoire ou suspension de paiement*, document prepared for the CADTM

Stiglitz, Joseph, *Globalization and Its discontents*, Penguin Books, 2002

— in *The New Republic*, 17 April 2000, see: <http://thenewrepublic.com/041700/stiglitz041700.html>

Tavernier, Yves, *International Monetary Fund, World Bank: vers une nuit du 4 août?*, Report on information from the Commission des Finances de l'Assemblée nationale on the workings of the IMF and the World Bank, no. 2801, Assemblée nationale, 2000

— *Fonds monétaire international, Banque mondiale: pour faire plaisir à Wall Street?*, Report on information from the Commission des Finances de l'Assemblée nationale on the workings of the IMF and the World Bank, no. 2801, Assemblée nationale, no. 3478, éd. Assemblée nationale, 2001

Tchangari, Moussa, 'Un projet néo-libéral pour l'Afrique', in *Alternative* (Niger), 24 July 2002

Toussaint, Éric, Une 'dette odieuse', in *Monde diplomatique*, February 2002

— *Your Money or Your Life: the Tyranny of Global Finance*, Pluto Press, 1998

Toussaint, Éric and Arnaud Zacharie, *Le bateau ivre de la mondialisation*, Syllepse/ CADTM, 2000

— *Afrique: abolir la dette pour libérer le développement*, Syllepse/ CADTM, 2001

— *Sortir de l'impasse, Dette et ajustement*, Syllepse/CADTM, 2002

UNDP, *Global Poverty Report 2000*

— *Human Development Report 2000*

— *Human Development Report 2002*

Verschave, François-Xavier, *L'envers de la dette*, Dossiers noirs 16, Agir Ici-Survie, Agone, 2001

— *Noir silence*, Les Arènes, 2000

World Bank, *Global Development Finance 2002*

— *World Development Indicators 2001*

Zacharie, Arnaud, *Dette écologique contre dette financière*, August 2002, *www.cadtm.org*

— *Sommet mondial de l'alimentation ou comment garantir un accès universel au gâteau*, June 2002 <www.cadtm.org>

Additional sources (in order of topics dealt with in the book)

Q2:

UNCTAD, *Least Developed Countries Report 2002*

FORBES, <www.forbes.com>

'PMA: toujours plus pauvres', *Jeune Afrique Économie*, no. 341, 18 June 2002

'La fièvre du paludisme consume l'Afrique', *Libération*, 25 April 2001

'Les pays pauvres isolés à la Conférence internationale sur le sida', *Les Échos*, 5–6 July 2002

'L'extrême pauvreté sous-estimée en Afrique', *Libération*, 19 June 2002

'Les OGM à l'assaut de l'Afrique', *L'Humanité*, 4 September 2002

OECD, *Official Development Assistance Statistics*, 2002

Q4:

FAO, *Situation des forêts du monde*, 2001 <www.fao.org>

'Le coût: 67% du budget santé du Mali', *Le Monde*, 27 August 2002

'Océans: le défi de la gouvernance', *Les Échos*, 8 July 2002

'Quatre dirigeants de grandes ONG témoignent', *L'Humanité*, 30 August 2002

Wolfensohn, James, 'Une chance pour le développement durable', in *Le Monde*, 23 August 2002

Q6:

Morel, Jacques, *Calendrier des crimes de la France outre-mer*, L'Esprit frappeur, 2001

Q7:

Agir Ici – Survie, *Dossiers noirs de la politique africaine en France no. 13*, L'Harmattan, 1999

Amis de la Terre, *Aides à l'exportation françaises: pour un développement durable et équitable* <www.amisdelaterre.org>

Q12–14:

Agir Ici – AITEC – CRID, *Comprendre les institutions financières internationales*, 1999

Amis de la Terre, *Guide citoyen du Fon* <www.amisdelaterre.org>

Q15:

Diago, Édouard, *Venezuela, pourquoi veulent-ils renverser Chavez ?*, in Critique Communiste, July 2002

Combat ouvrier, 20 April 2002, no. 858

Q17:

CADTM France, *Étude sur le Club de Paris*, 2002 <www.cadtm.org>

Q28:

'Le NEPAD peut-il réussir?', *Jeune Afrique Économie*, no. 341, 18 June 2002

'Est-ce vraiment le plan qu'il fallait à l'Afrique', *L'Autre Afrique*, no. 23, 3–16 July 2002

'Soutien verbal et … conditionnel', *L'Autre Afrique*, no. 24, 17–30 July 2002

'L'Afrique riche de ses pauvres', *Le Marabout*, no. 11–12, August–September 2002

NDIAYE Badara, *Le Nepad: un plan d'ajustement pour l'Afrique*, 2002 <www.cadtm.org>

Q29:

ROY Michaël, 'S'enrichir sur le dos des plus pauvres!', in *Le Courrier de Genève*, 23 December 2000

Q30:

Alliance pour un monde responsable, pluriel et solidaire, *chantier 9 Dette et ajustement*, November 2001

Q34:

'30 milliards de dollars du IMF pour le Brésil et la stabilité de l'Amérique latine', *Les Échos*, 9 August 2002

Q37:

'Glaciations sur le climat', *Libération*, 28 August 2002

'Terre: si rien n'est fait ...', *L'Autre Afrique*, no. 25, 31 July 2002

Q41:

'Deutsche Telekom songe à sortir des services informatiques', *Les Échos*, 9 July 2002

'France Telecom: le gouvernement se résout au départ de Michel Bon', *Les Échos*, 9 September 2002

'Worldcom avoue une fraude supplémentaire de 3,3 milliards de dollars', *Les Échos*, 12 August 2002

A Brave New Series

GLOBAL ISSUES
IN A CHANGING WORLD

This new series of short, accessible think-pieces deals with leading global issues of relevance to humanity today. Intended for the enquiring reader and social activists in the North and the South, as well as students, the books explain what is at stake and question conventional ideas and policies. Drawn from many different parts of the world, the series' authors pay particular attention to the needs and interests of ordinary people, whether living in the rich industrial or the developing countries. They all share a common objective – to help stimulate new thinking and social action in the opening years of the new century.

Global Issues in a Changing World is a joint initiative by Zed Books in collaboration with a number of partner publishers and non-governmental organizations around the world. By working together, we intend to maximize the relevance and availability of the books published in the series.

Participating NGOs

Both ENDS, Amsterdam
Catholic Institute for International Relations, London
Corner House, Sturminster Newton
Council on International and Public Affairs, New York
Dag Hammarskjöld Foundation, Uppsala
Development GAP, Washington DC
Focus on the Global South, Bangkok
IBON, Manila
Inter Pares, Ottawa
Public Interest Research Centre, Delhi
Third World Network, Penang
Third World Network–Africa, Accra
World Development Movement, London

About this Series

Communities in the South are facing great difficulties in coping with global trends. I hope this brave new series will throw much needed light on the issues ahead and help us choose the right options.

Martin Khor, Director, Third World Network, Penang

There is no more important campaign than our struggle to bring the global economy under democratic control. But the issues are fearsomely complex. This Global Issues series is a valuable resource for the committed campaigner and the educated citizen.

Barry Coates, Director, Oxfam New Zealand

Zed Books has long provided an inspiring list about the issues that touch and change people's lives. The Global Issues series is another dimension of Zed's fine record, allowing access to a range of subjects and authors that, to my knowledge, very few publishers have tried. I strongly recommend these new, powerful titles and this exciting series.

John Pilger, author

We are all part of a generation that actually has the means to eliminate extreme poverty world-wide. Our task is to harness the forces of globalization for the benefit of working people, their families and their communities – that is our collective duty. The Global Issues series makes a powerful contribution to the global campaign for justice, sustainable and equitable development, and peaceful progress.

Glenys Kinnock MEP

The Global Issues Series

Julian Burger, *First Peoples: What Future?*

Koen De Feyter, *Human Rights: Social Justice in the Age of the Market*

Susan Hawley and Morris Szeftel, *Corruption: Privatization, Transnational Corporations and the Export of Bribery*

Ann-Christin Sjölander Holland, *Water for Sale? Corporations against People*

Paola Monzini, *The Market in Women: Prostitution, Trafficking and Exploitation*

Roger Moody, *Digging the Dirt: The Modern World of Global Mining*

Edgar Pieterse, *City Futures: Confronting the Crisis of Urban Development*

Toby Shelley, *The Oil Industry: Politics, Poverty and the Planet*

Vivien Stern, *The Making of Crime: Prisons and People in a Market Society*

Nedd Willard, *The War on Drugs: Is This the Solution?*

For full details of this list and Zed's other subject and general catalogues, please write to: The Marketing Department, Zed Books, 7 Cynthia Street, London N1 9JF, UK or e-mail:

<sales@zedbooks.demon.co.uk>

Visit our website at <http://www.zedbooks.co.uk>

Participating Organizations

Both ENDS: A service and advocacy organization that collaborates with environment and indigenous organizations, both in the South and in the North, with the aim of helping to create and sustain a vigilant and effective environmental movement.

> Nieuwe Keizersgracht 45, 1018 VC Amsterdam, The Netherlands
> tel: +31 20 623 0823 fax: +31 20 620 8049
> e-mail: info@bothends.org
> website: www.bothends.org

Catholic Institute for International Relations (CIIR): CIIR aims to contribute to the eradication of poverty through a programme that combines advocacy at national and international level with community-based development.

> Unit 3 Canonbury Yard, 190a New North Road,
>   London N1 7BJ, UK
> tel: +44 (0)20 7354 0883 fax: +44 (0)20 7359 0017
> e-mail: ciir@ciir.org
> website: www.ciir.org

Corner House: The Corner House is a UK-based research and solidarity group working on social and environmental justice issues in North and South.

> PO Box 3137, Station Road, Sturminster Newton,
>   Dorset DT10 1YJ, UK
> tel: +44 (0)1258 473795 fax: +44 (0)1258 473748
> e-mail: cornerhouse@gn.apc.org
> website: www.cornerhouse.icaap.org

Council on International and Public Affairs (CIPA): CIPA is a human rights research, education and advocacy group, with a particular focus on economic and social rights in the USA and elsewhere around the world. Emphasis in recent years has been given to resistance to corporate domination.

> 777 United Nations Plaza, Suite 3c, New York, NY 10017, USA
> tel: +1 212 972 9877 fax: +1 212 972 9878

e-mail: cipany@igc.org
website: www.cipa-apex.org

Dag Hammarskjöld Foundation: The Dag Hammarskjöld Foundation, established in 1962, organizes seminars and workshops on social, economic and cultural issues facing developing countries, with a particular focus on alternative and innovative solutions. Results are published in its journal Develpment Dialogue.

Övre Slottsgatan 2, 753 10 Uppsala, Sweden.
tel: +46 18 102772 fax: +46 18 122072
e-mail: secretariat@dhf.uu.se
website: www.dhf.uu.se

Development GAP: The Development Group for Alternative Policies is a non-profit development resource organization working with popular organizations in the South and their Northern partners in support of a development that is truly sustainable and that advances social justice.

927 15th Street, nw, 4th Floor, Washington, DC 20005, USA
tel: +1 202 898 1566 fax: +1 202 898 1612
e-mail: dgap@igc.org
website: www.developmentgap.org

Focus on the Global South: Focus is dedicated to regional and global policy analysis and advocacy work. It works to strengthen the capacity of organizations of the poor and marginalized people of the South and to better analyse and understand the impacts of the globalization process on their daily lives.

c/o CUSRI, Chulalongkorn University, Bangkok 10330, Thailand
tel: +66 2 218 7363 fax: +66 2 255 9976
e-mail: admin@focusweb.org
website: www.focusweb.org

IBON: IBON Foundation is a research, education, and information institution that provides publications and services on socio-economic issues as support to advocacy in the Philippines and abroad. Through its research and databank, formal and non-formal education programs, media work, and international networking, IBON aims to build the capacity of both Philippine and international organizations.

Address: Rm. 303 SCC Bldg., 4427 Int. Old Sta. Mesa, Manila 1008
  Philippines
tel: +632 7132729, +632 7132737, +632 7130912
fax: +632 7160108
e-mail: editors@ibon.org
website: www.ibon.org

Inter Pares: Inter Pares, a Canadian social justice organization, has been active since 1975 in building relationships with Third World development groups and providing support for community-based development programmes. Inter Pares is also involved in education and advocacy in Canada, promoting understanding about the causes and effects of, and solutions to, poverty.

221 Laurier Ave East, Ottawa, Ontario, K1N 6P1 Canada
tel: + 1 613 563 4801 fax: + 1 613 594 4704
e-mail: info@interpares.ca
website: www.interpares.ca

Public Interest Research Centre: PIRC is a research and campaigning group based in Delhi that seeks to serve the information needs of activists and organizations working on macro-economic issues concerning finance, trade and development.

142, Maitri Apartments, Plot No. 28, Patparganj, Delhi: 110092,
  India
tel: + 91 11 2221081, 2432054 fax: + 91 11 2224233
e-mail: kaval@nde.vsnl.net.in

Third World Network: TWN is an international network of groups and individuals involved in efforts to bring about a greater articulation of the needs and rights of peoples in the Third World; a fair distribution of the world's resources; and forms of development that are ecologically sustainable and fulfil human needs. Its international secretariat is based in Penang, Malaysia.

121-S Julan Utama, 10450 Penang, Malaysia
tel: +60 4 226 6159 fax: +60 4 226 4505

e-mail: twnet@po.jaring.my
website: www.twnside.org.sg

Third World Network–Africa: TWN–Africa is engaged in research and advocacy on economic, environmental and gender issues. In relation to its current particular interest in globalization and Africa, its work focuses on trade and investment, the extractive sectors and gender and economic reform.

2 Ollenu Street, East Legon, PO Box an19452, Accra-North, Ghana.
tel: +233 21 511189/503669/500419 fax: +233 21 511188
e-mail: twnafrica@ghana.com

World Development Movement (WDM): The World Development Movement campaigns to tackle the causes of poverty and injustice. It is a democratic membership movement that works with partners in the South to cancel unpayable debt and break the ties of IMF conditionality, for fairer trade and investment rules, and for strong international rules on multinationals.

25 Beehive Place, London sw9 7QR, UK
tel: +44 (0)20 7737 6215 fax: +44 (0)20 7274 8232
e-mail: wdm@wdm.org.uk
website: www.wdm.org.uk

This book is also available in the following countries

CARIBBEAN
Ian Randle Publishers, 11 Cunningham Avenue, Box 686,
Kingston 6, Jamaica, W.I.
tel: (876) 978 0745, 978 0739 fax: 978 1158
e-mail: ianr@colis.com

EGYPT
MERIC (The Middle East Readers' Information Center)
2 Bahgat Ali Street, Tower D/Apt. 24, Zamalek, Cairo
tel: 20 2 735 3818/736 3824 fax: 20 2 736 9355

FIJI
University Book Centre, University of South Pacific, Suva
tel: 679 313 900 fax: 679 303 265

GHANA
EPP Book Services, P O Box TF 490, Trade Fair, Accra
tel: 233 21 773087 fax: 233 21 779099

MAURITIUS
Editions Le Printemps, 4 Club Road, Vacoas, Mauritius

MOZAMBIQUE
Sul Sensacoes, PO Box 2242, , Maputo
tel: 258 1 421974 fax: 258 1 423414

NAMIBIA
Book Den, PO Box 3469, Shop 4, Frans Indongo Gardens,
Windhoek
tel: 264 61 239976 fax: 264 61 234248

NEPAL
Everest Media Services, GPO Box 5443, Dillibazar,
Putalisadak Chowk, Kathmandu
tel: 977 1 416026 fax: 977 1 250176

NIGERIA
Mosuro Publishers, 52 Magazine Road, Jericho, Ibadan, Nigeria
tel: 234 2 241 3375   fax: 234 2 241 3374

PAKISTAN
Vanguard Books, 45 The Mall, Lahore
tel: 92 42 735 5079   fax: 92 42 735 5197

PAPUA NEW GUINEA
Unisearch PNG Pty Ltd, Box 320, University,
National Capital District
tel: 675 326 0130 fax: 675 326 0127

RWANDA
Librairie Ikirezi, PO Box 443,, Kigali
tel/fax: 250 71314

SUDAN
The Nile Bookshop, New Extension Street 41, P O Box 8036,
Khartoum
tel: 249 11 463 749

TANZANIA
TEMA Publishing Co Ltd, PO Box 63115, Dar Es Salaam
tel: 255 51 113608   fax: 255 51 110472

UGANDA
Aristoc Booklex Ltd, PO Box 5130, Kampala Road,
Diamond Trust Building, Kampala
tel/fax: 256 41 254867

ZAMBIA
UNZA Press, PO Box 32379, Lusaka
tel: 260 1 290409   fax: 260 1 253952

ZIMBABWE
Weaver Press, PO Box A1922, Avondale, Harare
tel: 263 4 308330   fax: 263 4 339645